RYAN C. GREENE
Foreword by Dr. Willie Jolley CSP, CPAE

Becoming A
*Passion*PRENEUR®

HOW TO TURN YOUR EXPERTISE INTO PROFITABLE,
CONTENT-BASED, PASSION-DRIVEN REVENUE STREAMS

BECOMING A PASSIONPRENEUR®
How to Turn Your Expertise Into Profitable, Content-Based, Passion-Driven Revenue Streams

Copyright ©2019, 2020 Ryan C. Greene. All Rights Reserved.
www.ryancgreene.com

Passionpreneur is a registered trademark of Ryan C. Greene. All unauthorized use is prohibited.

No part of this publication may be reproduced, stored in a retrieval system, or transmitted in any form by means electronic, mechanical, photocopying, recording or otherwise, except for the inclusion of brief quotations in a review, without prior permission in writing from the publisher.

Cover design by: GreeneHouse Media, Print Division

ISBN: 978-0-9842631-6-5

Printed in the USA

Published by
GreeneHouse Media

Dedication
To my beautiful, lovely and dedicated wife, Tyneka.
God blessed me with the most amazingly
perfect partner when he sent me you.
Thanks for being there with me "shooting in the gym".

TABLE OF CONTENTS

Endorsements

FOREWORD
Dr Willie Jolley

INTRODUCTION
13

THE PASSIONPRENEUR MINDSET
17

Take The Passionpreneur Assessment
The Passionpreneur Matrix
Stop Grinding and Start Building
Start Setting S.T.U.P.I.D. Goals
Get Paid For What You KNOW
Please Don't Quit Your Day Job (Yet)!

RE-IGNITE YOUR FIRE WITHIN
51

10 Surefire Ways To Re-Ignite Your Fire Within

9 BUSINESS MYTHS THAT ARE KEEPING YOU BROKE
71

Myth #1:   You Earned It So You Deserve To Spend It
Myth #2:   Your Job Is Enough
Myth #3:   This Is As Good As It Gets
Myth #4:   The Money Is In The List
Myth #5:   If It's Gonna Get Done Right, You Have To Do It
Myth #6:   No One Is Going To Pay YOU That Much Money
Myth #7:   Fake It 'Til You Make It
Myth #8:   Mindset Is All You Need To Succeed
Myth #9:   If You Share Your Dream Someone Will Steal It

BECOMING A PASSIONPRENEUR
89

Secret #1:   Get Paid For What You Know, Not For What You Do
Secret #2:   Pursue Your Passion
Secret #3:   Chase Purpose Not Profits
Secret #4:   Give Give Give!!!!
Secret #5:   The Fierce Urgency Of NOW
Secret #6:   Fire Yourself And Hire Systems
Secret #7:   Live Your Story, Tell Your Story

THE PASSIONPRENEUR PRODUCT MATRIX
113
How To Create Your Passion-Driven Revenue Streams

CONCLUSION
135

PASSIONPRENEUR BONUS RESOURCES
139
6 Cornerstones To Building Your Business Upon A Strong Foundation
How To Set S.T.U.P.I.D. Goals Worksheet
The Passionpreneur Pyramid Worksheet
The Passionpreneur Product Matrix

MEET "THE PASSIONPRENEUR"
143

FOREWORD

I've spoken on stages all over the world. I've motivated crowds of all nationalities, ethnicities, and cultures. I've spoken to college students and college presidents, executive assistants and chief executive officers. No matter who the audience, no matter what their challenge, the one common denominator in the lives of the most successful people I've encountered is an undying, unwavering passion for the work they do.

When Ryan approached me about penning the foreword for this powerful book <u>Becoming A Passionpreneur</u> I got excited that FINALLY someone was taking the next step in elevating the conversation about passion and how to actually build a successful business around it. Some people talk about passion but are not passionate. And some others are passionate but never share how they got there. Yet, Ryan has both parts covered.

"Pursuing your passion" has become almost cliché in the personal development space. Passion speakers seem to be a dime a dozen. But what Ryan has done in this book, is he's given readers a tangible step by step blueprint on 1) How to re-ignite your passion for those who have lost it, 2) How to transform your mindset into that of a Passionpreneur, and 3) How to build your passion-driven business TODAY.

In my book *Turn Setbacks Into Greenbacks*, I teach on how to go from financial devastation to financial freedom. It doesn't matter where you presently are financially, it only takes persistence, hunger, and determination to power through your tough times to better days. When Ford Motor Company called me in 2006 to speak to their employees in hopes of getting 25,000 of them to quit their jobs and take the buyout, I went in not with the goal of getting employees to quit, but with the goal of simply getting them to dream bigger. I wanted them to realize there was more to life than the jobs they had planned to work for 40 years until retirement. After speaking to them, over 38,000 employees took the buyout and bet on themselves.

I see this project by Ryan in the same vein. Becoming a Passionpreneur requires you to dream bigger. It requires you to believe in yourself. It requires you to accept that you were created to do more than build someone else's dream. This book gives you permission to pursue your own dreams and generate revenue in your own way. This project is going to challenge you to tap into areas in yourself you forgot about and have placed on the back burner for far too long. You don't have to quit your job to become a Passionpreneur, but you may have to quit some bad habits as well as be willing to put in some hard work.

Success isn't easy. This book isn't a magic pill or get rich quick scheme. You will have to put in the work to see the results. The wonderful thing is Ryan has put together a system, that when followed, will have you living your most profitable and passionate life imaginable. What I love most about this book is he didn't just rely on his own knowledge and experiences, but he's tapped the insights of so many other

Passionpreneurs who are making a living by living their passions every day. Their stories featured in this book as well as the interviews featured online are such a priceless resource all by itself.

I'm excited to be a part of this powerful project. Anytime I can be a part of a project that empowers others to create better versions of themselves and live their most fulfilled lives, I'm in. Ryan is not just teaching this stuff, he's living it. We even attend the same church so I know his heart and character are genuine. I'm excited about the work he's doing and the thousands of Passionpreneurs who will be birthed from this project.

Dr. Willie Jolley, CSP, CPAE

Best Selling Author of <u>A Setback Is A Setup For A Comeback</u> & <u>Turn Setbacks Into Greenback</u> and Host of the "Willie Jolley Wealthy Ways Show" on Sirius XM

INTRODUCTION

Hold your hand on your belly. Do you feel that? Press harder. No? Nothing? Do you remember when there used to be a fire there? When a burning desire inside of you that drove your every action once resided in the depth of your belly? Remember that feeling? All that's left now is the smoldering ruins of what used to be your purpose, passion and dreams. The raging inferno that once fueled your life was left to become but a dim flicker and you've settled for a life of "good enough". What happened? Where did your fire go? Why did you let it die? More importantly, how do you re-ignite it?

We've all been there at some point in our lives. Anyone who lives a life of purpose and has ever chased a dream has at some point faced seasons of doubt, discomfort and darkness. Wanting to give up is a very real challenge. Pushing through times of lack and little motivation isn't a foreign concept to those who are striving to achieve the highest calling on their lives. It's just a fact of life that at some point, everyone's fire fades along the journey. The difference in those who end up living a mediocre mundane life and those who live a fantastically fulfilled life is how they push through those periods and re-ignite their fire within.

So, what happens when your fire goes out? How do you light the flames again? That's what this book is designed to help you do. This book will give you the tools you need to re-ignite your fire within and make a living doing what you love, by building passion-driven revenue streams. Look at this book as your accelerant as well as your matches. As your coach, it is my pledge to get you back on fire about life and back on fire about your passion, purpose and dreams! The journey won't be easy, but it will be abundantly worth it. Together we can get you on the road to becoming a PASSIONPRENEUR!

If you've ever read one of my previous books or followed me at all, you may be asking "Ryan, what do you know about losing your passion? You're always up to something. Whether writing books, producing seminars, or developing new radio shows, your fire always seems to be burning." Admit it, you were asking me that, right? Well the truth is, even in the midst of all the public activity you may see, there's been many a battle I've had to fight within myself to keep encouraged and excited about doing all that I do.

In my last book (Part 2 of the Purpose, Power & Passion Series) <u>Create A Better YOU!</u> I talked about going through my divorce and how that wiped me out emotionally and creatively for almost five years. I spent a lot of time aimlessly going through the motions of pursuing my dreams and even flat out quitting several times. I've been there, but I didn't STAY there. This book is my offering to the world, my offering to you, on just what I continue to do even now to keep my fire burning. Hopefully these lessons will help you to re-ignite your own fire as well.

Successful people aren't successful because they always got it right along the way. They're not successful because they never faced challenges and quit. Successful people are successful because even in their darkest hour, when their destiny seemed to be most out of reach, they buckled down and found a way to stay the course and continue toward their ultimate goal. Quitting is not that unnatural and wanting to give up is not that foreign a concept when you are pursuing something great. The key factor however, separating those who succeed and those who fail is the innate desire to start back up after you have quit.

Let's take this journey together. For the next few hundred pages and however many days it takes you to read this book, let's go through this process I've laid out and get you back on track. I want to see you excited about pursuing dreams and fulfilling your purpose again. I want to see you walk away with a solid plan of how you are going to create passion-driven revenue streams and make a living doing what you love.

It's time to take back control of your thoughts, actions and environment in order to get you on fire again about everything you wish to do and become. As usual, I'll share several personal stories about my own journey down this road and how I was able to bounce back and re-ignite my fire. Through my stories you will see that your journey is not unlike anyone else's and you too can overcome. You too can become a PASSIONPRENEUR.

There will be some spiritual talk, some practical talk, some personal life, and some business life talk along the way. There is one main ingredient necessary for this journey- you must take accountability and own your role in all of this. You must be willing to work and do the things I teach you in order to see the change take place. I've been doing this a long time. My first book was released in 2006. I'm not really interested in writing books to make you say things like "Wow that was profound. That brother is deep!". My purpose is to see my books and teachings positively change your life based on you applying the principles I teach. Don't TELL me "Ryan, that book was so on point!" SHOW me how on point it is by letting me see the changes in your life once you go apply the lessons and re-ignite your fire within and pursue your passions.

So, if you're ready to live your life with purpose, live your life with power and live your life with passion, let's get started! If you're ready to live a more fulfilled life doing what you love, let's get started! If you're ready to put your passions to work, get paid for what you know, and become a PASSIONPRENEUR, let's get started!

THE PASSIONPRENEUR MINDSET

*"You must see a shift in your mindset,
before you can see a shift in your paycheck."*

One day I was shopping at my local grocery store and one cashier said to another "Yes! It's 12:17." The other cashier asked what she was so excited about. The first cashier said she was excited because she gets off at 4pm. She was at work and all she could think about was getting off of work. I was a customer in her line and while she was supposed to be focused on serving me, while the store was paying her to work for them, while so many other people out there wished they could have her job, the only thing on her mind was leaving for the day.

As crazy as it was to me, I wasn't even shocked because so many of us fall into the same trap. We fall into the trap where the only thing we're excited about when we're at work is getting off from work! How many people go work every day and actually hate what they do? People will go to a job for 8, 10, sometimes even 12 hours, and the thing they're most motivated about at work is getting off work when their time is up. They watch the clock all day waiting to go home where they may spend 4-5 hours on average living their life doing the things that make them happy. Then they go to bed, wake up the next morning, and do it all again.

A 2018 Gallup Poll showed almost 70% of U.S. employees are either disengaged or actively disengaged at work. SEVENTY PERCENT! Seven out of every 10 employees are getting up every morning, getting dressed every morning, sitting in traffic every morning, greeting co-workers every morning, working full shifts every day, sitting in traffic going home every evening, for a job in which they're not even engaged! And we wonder why people seem so angry everywhere we go? Uhh… probably because they hate what they're doing and wish they could be doing something else.

We live in communities full of people who are unfulfilled by the work they do. We live in communities full of people who would much rather be working on projects that excite them and give them purpose. Some hide it better than others. Some adapt better than others. Others release that pain upon every single person they cross. So many around us feel captive by their financial, social, professional, and familial circumstances. They feel they have too much to lose. They know that while they hate their situation, they can't afford to take the risk to change it.

Does that person sound familiar to you? Sound like someone you know? Let me be more direct. Does that person sound like YOU? I'm going to go out on a limb and say since you're reading this book (unless you bought it just because you thought the cover was dope) you probably have felt these feelings at some point. Fret not, as I said earlier, so have 70% of all Americans. You are not alone. The great thing for you, however, is you now have a roadmap to help you make a living doing what you love by building passion-driven revenue streams.

This book, like all my other books, starts with me first. I'm writing this book because I lived this book. I've gone through everything I'm discussing and teaching, and through it all, discovered how to become a Passionpreneur and find joy in the work I do. First and foremost, I want you to understand this- this book is not about quitting your job! While this book, and becoming a Passionpreneur, is about generating new revenue streams through your passions, the plan is to learn how to do that while still working your job.

This is a roadmap to generating automated income doing that thing you've always felt a passion to do but didn't know how to create revenue doing it. Trust me, I've quit my job too soon chasing a dream and there's nothing fun about that! More on that later in the chapter though. Becoming a Passionpreneur is all about living a more fulfilled life by learning how to generate income doing what you love. It's a means by which one can give themselves options in life. While you very well may be able to replace your income one day, the true purpose of becoming a Passionpreneur is to 1) help you do the thing you're most passionate about doing so that your life feels more fulfilling. 2) help you generate a new automated revenue stream so that you don't feel so imprisoned by your job and current financial situation. 3) help you create true freedom and options for your life.

I shared the story about the grocery store that sparked the idea for this book, but the concept was birthed even before that awesome cashier who helped me. As a professional speaker and author, I've been blessed to travel the country and meet all types of people in all walks of life. The one comment I get the most, from cashiers to CPAs, is "I just wish I had more time/resources/will to go after what I really dream of doing." Without question, the one thing I've learned that keeps people disengaged, disgruntled, and dissatisfied, is they find themselves stuck doing what they have to do, instead of doing what they want to do. They all have long-term dreams that at some point they pushed to the side in order to fulfill some immediate short-term goals. Along the way, those short-term goals took over and became their every day way of life and those dreams began to die.

My mission with this book, with every talk I give, with The Passionpreneur® Podcast, and so on, is to help people rekindle their passions, reclaim their purpose, and revive their dreams. I want to see people more fulfilled with their lives and thereby happier as they go day to day. I honestly believe that if that person with road rage flipping you the bird, was actually excited about the job they were heading to, they wouldn't be so angry behind the wheel. If that customer service rep was truly passionate about their job and not just their because they couldn't afford to quit, you would have a much more pleasant experience at [insert every company name here] when you shopped.

The bottom line is people aren't happy. Those 70% disengaged employees have a very tangible negative impact on our daily lives. How much more productive would companies be, how much more pleasant would our overall experiences be, if those 70%ers (yes, you included) were working in their purpose and pursuing their passions, as opposed to working a job they feel they can't afford to leave for whatever number of reasons? Becoming a Passionpreneur gives you a freedom unlike any you've ever experienced. There's a peace of mind and a joy that comes from doing a work you love and are passionate about.

So, let's get into it. Let's start this journey to becoming a Passionpreneur. This book is broken down into several sections. This first section is going to deal with the mindset of becoming a Passionpreneur. Then we will get into how to re-ignite your fire within and get you excited about that which you're called to do and love to do. After that, we'll tackle some stinking thinking as we destroy business myths that you may have heard but will do nothing but hinder your progress. Then we will begin the journey of learning the secrets to generating passion-driven revenue streams and developing your

Passionpreneur Plan and how to get you started on your journey to becoming a PASSIONPRENEUR!

I probably should have warned you sooner, but this book is going to require you to work. It is a living document that only has value when you do what's required for each section. Sure, I could wax eloquently with the most impassioned prose and impress statesmen and scholars alike with my erudite presentation, but lord would that be a bore and how would that help anyone? So yes, we're in this thing together. I'm speaking to YOU and together we're going to make this journey both exciting and life changing. So, let's go!

Read the following quotes three times each:

"Hard work is a prison sentence only if it does not have meaning."
~ Malcolm Gladwell

"Your work is going to fill a large part of your life, and the only way to be truly satisfied is to do what you believe is great work. And the only way to do great work is to love what you do" ~ Steve Jobs

Answer the following questions:

I am most happy when I am able to

_____

_____

_____

_____

If I could do one thing for the rest of my life I would

_____

_____

My true passion is

_____

_____

Hopefully, you've answered the preceding questions truthfully and put some real thought into your answers. Your answers will serve as your guiding star on this journey. A few years ago, I made a commitment that I would no longer do any worker for which I was not truly passionate. Understand, I didn't say I wasn't going to work. A man gotta eat, right? But my declaration was that I was no longer going to settle for work solely for the sake of a paycheck. My work had to matter, and my work had to make an impact. By the end of this book, we will have an entire business designed around your passion and expertise, with everything you need to start generating automated passion-driven revenue.

TAKE THE PASSIONPRENEUR ASSESSMENT

Before we go much further, it's important to assess if you are ready to become a Passionpreneur. This quick 15 question assessment will serve as a tool to see where you are right now and if this is even the type of journey you want to take. Entrepreneurship isn't for everyone. Determining your level of aptitude to embark upon this journey will be quite helpful. Don't worry, you're not taking the LSAT. There are no right or wrong answers. The assessment is simply designed to see how you think about certain things. Take a few minutes to complete your answers below.

**The Passionpreneur Assessment:
Are You Ready To Pursue A Passion-Driven Business?**
How do you rank yourself in each of these areas on a scale of 1-10?

	1	2	3	4	5	6	7	8	9	10
I am clear on my life's purpose and am living it.										
I am following my passion and love going to work every day.										
I use my passion to improve my life and the lives of others.										
I am confident in my own abilities to achieve.										
I act on my dreams and goals daily.										
I am living my desired lifestyle.										
I have a clear, written WHY that guides my actions.										
If money weren't an issue, I would work my current profession for free.										
I am not afraid to take risks.										
I actively help others pursue their purpose and passion.										
I am currently working in my passion.										
I keep a positive mental attitude and inspire others to do the same.										
I am totally fulfilled in my current profession.										
I am driven to achieve more each day.										
I make time to pursue my passion no matter what my circumstances look like.										

Add up your score. How did you rank?

15 – 60: You may feel that you aren't living a passion-driven life, but don't despair. There are many resources to help you find your passion. Find a coach or take some classes that will help you in the areas where

you are weak. Request feedback from those with whom you regularly work to see what they feel you can do to become more passion-driven. Following your passion in life is a NOT a spectator sport. The only way you improve in business is to get coaching and incorporate the feedback you receive.

61 – 100: You are well on your way to living a passion-driven life. Consider enrolling in a business bootcamp or training in order to gain the necessary help you need to push you over the top.

101 – 140: You have made significant strides in living a passion-driven life. Focus on strengthening those areas that you scored the lowest in so that you can truly become a Passion-Driven Leader.

141 – 150: You are a ready to become a Passionpreneur! Make sure that you continue to take advantage of opportunities to increase your skills.

THE PASSIONPRENEUR MATRIX

On the road to becoming a Passionpreneur, you may find yourself in any one of four quadrants. Each quadrant is like a different level of enlightenment and achievement. The journey from level to level is similar to that of a padawan growing into a full Jedi. There's no inherent good or bad to any of the quadrants per say; however, there's only one quadrant where true Passionpreneurs reside. Finding yourself in the first three quadrants while calling yourself a Passionpreneur will ultimately prove detrimental to your growth and development. I would go deeper with the Star Wars/Jedi analogy, but I've only seen Episodes IV-VI so I'll save myself the embarrassment of trying to sound hip. So, let's just move on.

Quadrant 1: Little Talent + Little Passion = POINTLESS

	Little Passion	Lots of Passion
Little Talent	POINTLESS	
Lots of Talent		

You will find yourself in this quadrant when you are trying to build something that you have little talent to do and you lack any passion about the thing. At this stage you're pointless to everyone. You're not going to convince anyone to build something you don't even enjoy doing. Even more, you won't find much success trying to operate in an arena where you lack the required talent to excel. People find themselves in the POINTLESS Quadrant when they focus on chasing a check or the next hot thing. There's an abundant means by which you can make money in this world. Choosing the right means for YOU is the only way to become a successful Passionpreneur.

Pointless people don't stick around long. There's a saying that "time will either promote or expose you" and once pointless people get exposed, they shift to another quadrant. If you're working a job in which you lack the talent to succeed and lack the passion for the job, either you will make the decision to walk away, or your boss will be kind enough to help you move on.

Quadrant 2: Lots of Talent + Little Passion = PRETENDER

	Little Passion	Lots of Passion
Little Talent	POINTLESS	
Lots of Talent	PRETENDER	

Have you ever heard the term "Renaissance (Wo)Man" or "Jack of All Trades?? It's what they call people who are skilled in multiple areas. Many of us find that there are several things we do well. Most athletes are great in multiple sports. Many musicians can play multiple instruments. Many creatives excel in multiple areas of creativity. But just because you are equally talented enough to perform multiple jobs or skills, doesn't mean you're necessarily equally passionate about each of them.

For instance, I am skilled at building websites. When people see websites I've built, they ask me to build sites for them. The problem is I HATE building websites. I have the talent to build sites, but I lack the passion and desire to make that a business I'd want to build. I've seen far too many entrepreneurs fall into the trap of becoming PRETENDERS and investing their time, money, and lives into building something they're good at, but hate doing, all because outside people convinced them that's where their skillset should take them.

Parents, yes, I'm talking to you, stop pushing your kids into becoming pretenders before they even have a chance to discover their passions. Just because your kid can assemble thousand-piece Lego® sets in 45 minutes, doesn't automatically mean she wants to be an engineer and miss summer vacation to go to Young Engineers of America Camp. Just because Little Ashton enjoys playing catch with you during the weekend, doesn't mean he wants to go pro and join spring, summer, and fall baseball leagues. Talent without passion breeds pretenders. They'll go along with your plan until they find their true passion and break your heart when they say all those years of piano lessons you paid for are down the tube because they really want to be a welder.

Remember those 70% of disengaged workers I mentioned earlier in the book? This is where they are. The world is full of a lot of talented people, doing work they couldn't care less about. Just dreaming and praying for a change and a way out. If you find yourself in this Pretender Quadrant, hopefully you will be inspired to shift right away.

Quadrant 3: Little Talent + Lots of Passion = PROMOTER

	Little Passion	Lots of Passion
Little Talent	POINTLESS	PROMOTER
Lots of Talent	PRETENDER	

Have you ever had a passion for something that you weren't personally good at doing? I know I love the game of football. As a kid in Baltimore with no pro team during the 80's and early 90's (Thanks Indianapolis), my favorite NFL Team was The Philadelphia Eagles. I wore a ¾ length green Triple Fat Goose Eagles coat all through middle school. I cried when Jerome Brown died. I just knew I was going to be Randall Cunningham when I grew up! I played all four years in high school and by senior year I was the starting quarterback and captain of the team.

My freshman year in college at Hampton University, I tried out for spring ball and made the football team as a walk-on. It was that spring that it finally hit me. No matter how much I loved the game, I wasn't really that good at playing quarterback. Shoot, I wasn't really that good at football all together. I wasn't a scrub, but I certainly wasn't good enough to ever see playing time on a college team.

For me it was football. For you it may be something else. What do you do when you're passionate about something, but not good at it? One option you have is to enter the PROMOTER Quadrant. In the Promoter Quadrant, you are able to work in your area of passion without you being the talent. What does that look like? Think about the sports anchor on ESPN who was never talented enough to play basketball but loves the game enough to learn all about it and become an expert analyst in it. Or the person who loves making music but cannot sing so they become a songwriter, label owner, or artist manager. There's plenty of opportunity to prosper from the role of a promoter. Don King never fought a fight himself, yet he is one of boxing's most successful promoters of all time.

It takes a big person to admit they don't have what it takes to be the star and fall back and be the cheerleader from someone else. Being the promoter allows you to still work around what you love, but from a different vantage point than you may have originally imagined. Industries wouldn't survive without promoters. Can you imagine if everyone in Hollywood was trying to be actors? Who would direct and produce? Who would write screenplays? Who would be the key grips? There is great value and earning potential in being a promoter; but the work is plenty, and the laborers are few. The world is full of far more pretenders than promoters. So many pretenders could be making a real difference if they shifted their mindset and moved to being promoters.

Quadrant 4: Lots of Talent + Lots of Passion = PASSIONPRENEUR

	Little Passion	Lots of Passion
Little Talent	POINTLESS	PROMOTER
Lots of Talent	PRETENDER	**PASSIONPRENEUR**

This is the pinnacle you seek. When you find the thing which you have lots of talent in AND you have lots of passion for it, now you can begin exploring the ways of becoming a Passionpreneur. Building a business, even a part-time passion-driven business is difficult. It takes hard work, perseverance, and determination among many other things. If you are going to commit any time and resources to building any type of business, why wouldn't you build one which you are most passionate about?

Later in the book, we will do an exercise to explore both the talents you've been blessed with, as well as the passions that lie within you. That's the foundation of becoming a Passionpreneur. That's Quadrant 4. That's the thesis of this book. Making a living doing what you love by building passion-driven revenue streams. The only way to become a true Passionpreneur is by building around your talents you're most passionate about.

Like I said earlier, I'm a talented web designer. But I have zero passion about web design. I am passionate about football. But I have little talent for the game. What am I both talented at and passionate about doing? Writing, speaking, and coaching entrepreneurs. And guess what. That's exactly the businesses I launched. If you look now at my website www.ryancgreene.com you will see I write books, provide coaching courses, and speak on those subjects. My business is a passion-driven business and therefore it never feels like work. That's where I want to get you. By the end of the book, you will have your roadmap and strategy for building your own passion-driven business.

Take a look one more time at the completed Passionpreneur Matrix.

	Little Passion	Lots of Passion
Little Talent	POINTLESS	PROMOTER
Lots of Talent	PRETENDER	PASSIONPRENEUR

If you're honest with yourself, in which quadrant are you currently operating? Are you Pointless, a Pretender, a Promoter, or a Passionpreneur? I'm going to assume since this book is entitled

"Becoming A Passionpreneur" and you're still reading it, that you want to move to the Passionpreneur Quadrant. Let's discuss best ways to build to that level and how to set goals to get you there.

BUILD UPON A STRONG FOUNDATION

I decided back in 2015, that I was no longer going to use the word "grind" in relation to my business. You probably have heard entrepreneurs say they're grinding in their business. It's almost as if it is some badge of honor. Entrepreneurs, hustlers, dreamers, proudly proclaim they're grinding to show they are working on building their empire. Well, I believe words have power and should be chosen wisely so I stopped "grinding".

It's time to stop grinding in your business and start BUILDING your business. To grind means to "reduce to small particles". To grind at something you're trying to build is like trying to run a 100-yard dash on ice. When any two things grind against each other, there is pain, discomfort, and destruction. When you build, you "construct by putting parts together over time upon strong foundation". Every successful business must be built upon a strong foundation. The foundation is the lowest load-bearing part of any building. It's often unseen but it's most important. There are many professionals who have great skills, talents, products, services etc., but they have no foundation. They seemingly come out of nowhere and take the industry by storm, but before you know it, they're out of business and on to the next thing. Becoming a Passionpreneur and building your business for longevity will require you to focus on six cornerstones that will help you build your business upon a strong foundation.

Here are those 6 cornerstones:

1. SCOPE (What is your mission?)

Everyone goes into business with the hopes of making a profit; however, your business must have a greater mission than simply making money. Who are you serving? Who are you seeking to help? Why did you create your product or service? Those questions should drive your company's actions, not simply increasing revenue. When money is the sole driver in your business, you will easily steer off course at every opportunity to make more of it. When you are driven by your mission, it keeps you focused on the true reasons you started your business in the first place.

2. SUPPORT (Who's on your team?)

If massive success is one of your goals then you're going to need a team, a squad. First, start with your Mastermind Group. These are your Idea People. They make you better by the brain capital they bring to the table. Next, you are going to need your Doers. They will be the ones who bring your great ideas to life. Thirdly, you need Ambassadors. These are the people who are going to be your public cheerleaders and help spread the word of how great your company is. People are your greatest resource. The more you have on board, the more momentum your company will build.

3. SYSTEMS (How do things get done?)

Systems are ways to do the job the same way every time (preferably without anyone having to physically do it each time). The better your systems, the better your business. A few systems you need in place include: CRM systems for managing customers and projects, sales systems to generate revenue, product delivery systems that give your clients what you promised, marketing systems that generate new prospects continually, and follow up systems that keep your company in front of prospects and clients. We'll go deeper into what these systems look like later in the book.

4. SCALABILITY (Are you ready today for tomorrow's growth?)

You can't wait until your company needs to grow to begin planning for that growth. From Day One you should be planning for growth and how you are going to handle it as a company. If you get a huge order, how are you going to fill it? If you get some sudden publicity, can your website handle the traffic? Don't lose business over your lack of planning ahead of time for success.

5. SELF AWARENESS (Know who you are and be THAT!)

Know what your competition is doing but always be YOU. Excel at the things you do best and crush it in those areas. Don't allow your business to suffer an identity crisis by trying to copy every new fad you see the competition doing. Consistency beats creativity every time. Customers look for businesses they can count on to deliver. Become the best in your field in what you're best at doing and let that be your calling card in the marketplace.

6. SUSTAINABILITY (Are you building to last?)

A true business stands the test of time. Make sure you are taking care of all the invisible business killers (legal coverage, insurance, taxes) so that your business is here to stay. Make decisions that will position you to be in business for decades to come and not a fly-by-night company. The future is coming whether you plan for it or not, so you might as well plan.

START SETTING S.T.U.P.I.D. GOALS

Goal setting. It's one of the cornerstones of any success blueprint. Every professional has been through some level of goal setting training. Who hasn't been taught how to set S.M.A.R.T. goals a hundred times in their career? It's become one of those concepts that we all know is critical, yet we seem to also take for granted.

Think about the last big goals you set. Did you achieve those goals, or did you quit? Why do so many of us give up on our goals that once meant so much to us when we were crafting them? If we're setting S.M.A.R.T. goals, you know, specific, measurable, action-oriented, realistic, time-sensitive goals, then why do so many of us continue to fall short on achieving them? More importantly, why do so many of us not even care when we do?

That's the quandary I searched to solve when I created S.T.U.P.I.D. Goals. Just like S.MA.R.T. goals, S.T.U.P.I.D. goals is an acronym. Each letter stands for an important element necessary for setting goals that will be impossible for you to quit. S.T.U.P.I.D goals fill in the missing elements of effective goal setting and help you plan for obstacles before you begin. When you know what to expect and how to better deal with the roadblocks you'll inevitably face along the way, you will have far greater success in achieving your goals.

So, what are S.T.U.P.I.D Goals? Let's get to it!

SACRIFICE: *What are you willing to give up to achieve your goal?*

Knowing what you are willing to give up before you get started is the most critical part of setting goals you won't quit on before completing. Far too often, leaders set great goals on paper without ever contemplating the true price it will take to achieve it. You need to know going in just how much time, money, family time, travel, late nights, and more, it will take to achieve your goal. Are you willing to miss the kid's recitals and date night with your spouse in order to achieve your goal? How much money are you willing to sink into your idea before you decide "enough is enough"? You don't want to wait until you're deep into your journey to then realize the road is too rough for you to tread. Before you embark upon your goals, take an honest inventory of all the necessary sacrifices your goal requires and decide if you're willing to give up those things in order to achieve them.

TEAM: *Who is going to help you achieve your goal?*

John C. Maxwell said, "No great accomplishment was ever achieved by one person alone." Any goal worth achieving is going to require a team who helps you achieve it. Don't wait until your back is against the wall to then start trying to find help. Expect upfront to need other people to help you be great. People are you #1 resource in business and leadership. The weak leader says, "If it's going to get done right, I have to do it myself." The stronger leader asks, "Who do I know who can do this task better than me?"

UPLIFTING: *Where is your goal taking you that's better than now?*

What good is a goal if it doesn't take you to a higher level in some area of your life? The whole purpose of setting goals is because there's something out there that's better than what you have, somewhere out there that's better than where you are, someone out there who's better than who you are. The pitfall most goal setting exercises fall into is they never force you to explicitly articulate and illustrate what that thing is. If there's some level you're trying to achieve, you need to as vividly and explicitly as possible articulate that when setting your goals. Being able to look at that new level and see it before you reach it, will motivate you in ways unimaginable during the tough times. It's that aspiration that will drive you when you want to quit. If you don't have that written out, you'll find yourself quitting every time the road gets rough.

PLAN: *How do you plan to achieve your goal?*

"He who fails to plan, plans to fail." That quote is attributed to Winston Churchill with a little ghostwriting from Benjamin Franklin. "Poor execution will kill even the greatest of ideas". That quote is attribute to ME. (Did you peep that double entendre?) Your goal is only as strong as your plan to achieve it. Here's why your team is so vital. You won't have all the answers. If you think you do have all the answers, I can assure you they're not all the best answers. Collaboration trumps isolation all day. Don't confuse your "plan" with your "strategy" or your "tools". Your PLAN is the detailed day-by-day measurable activities you will use to reach your goal. Your strategy is the means by which you will accomplish your plan. Your tools are the specific things you use to implement your strategy. So, your plan may be to reach 1,000 new prospects in the next six months. Your strategy may be to do a daily online social media blitz. Your tools would then be Facebook, Twitter, and Instagram. Too often I see people confuse their tools with their plan. "Facebook" is not a plan, it's a tool.

INSPIRED: *Why are you going after your goal?*

Inspired is not to be confused with Uplifting. When discussing making sure your goal is uplifting, it was more about WHERE you want to go. When discussing making sure your goals are inspired, this is about understanding WHY you want to go there. If your why is big enough, the how will figure itself out. Every goal you set must have a strong level of inspiration behind it or else why would you even pursue it? When determining your inspiration for your goals, I'd challenge you to do a few things. First, use something you can be proud of and enjoy as your inspiration. Secondly, make it about someone other than yourself. It's much easier to quit on yourself than it is to quit on someone who's counting on you. Maybe it's your kids, maybe your spouse or parents, maybe it's your team, or maybe it's total strangers who will benefit from your achievement. Finally, find inspiration that will make you cry if you quit. If the thought of quitting on your goal doesn't bring real tears to your eyes, then your why isn't big enough and your goal isn't as inspired as it could be.

DEADLINE: *When do you plan to achieve your goal?*

We've covered the Who, What, Where, How, and Why and all that's left is the When. Every goal needs to have a deadline attached. A goal without a deadline is simply a dream. You must set a date and push for it. A 90-Day Blitz. A 24-Hour Marathon. Lose 15 pounds in 30 days. It doesn't matter the goal, if there's no deadline attached, it's a pointless venture. There's something about knowing in your mind that something must get done by a certain date. Pareto's 80/20 Rule speaks to the idea that 80% of any task gets done in the last 20% of the time. If that's true, and I believe it is, then it's important to set that deadline so that your 80% kicks in. Think about how much more powerful "My goal is to lose 15 pounds in the next 30 days." sounds over "My goal is to lose 15 pounds." See the difference? Martin Luther King, Jr. talked about "the fierce urgency of now". When accomplishing goals, a deadline builds in an automatic fierce urgency which pushes us to action.

Get a copy of "Setting S.T.U.P.I.D. Goals" Audio Training for FREE.

Setting goals is critical to your success, but your success is measured by actually achieving those goals you set. When you begin setting S.T.U.P.I.D. goals, it will become impossible for you to quit on your goals because you've now set goals based on what truly matters to you and moves you. It's my goal to see more people set goals that work for them so they can achieve the success they desire. That being said, I don't want you to simply have this information. I want you to read it and apply it to your life right away. **You can get a FREE copy of my audio download "Setting S.T.U.P.I.D. Goals" by texting the word GOALS to (614) 333-0338.** You will receive an audio download as well as a "Setting S.T.U.P.I.D. Goals" Worksheet for you to begin setting your goals today.

GET PAID FOR WHAT YOU KNOW, NOT FOR WHAT YOU DO

Since 2008, in my book *My Little Black Book of Leadership*, I have stressed one very important idea about maximizing your profitability and earning potential. The idea is that you should always strive to get paid for what you KNOW, not for what you DO. The wealthiest, and most fulfilled, people don't trade their time for money. They trade their MIND for money. When you are getting paid for things you do, you are always replaceable by the next person, machine, or system that can do what you do better, faster, and cheaper. Just look at almost every retail store. Look at all the self-checkout lines that have replaced human cashiers. Those cashiers were getting paid to do a task. Once those above them discovered a better way to ring up customers, they got rid of cashiers and had customers ring up themselves- for free!

The managers who figured getting rid of cashiers in lieu of self-checkouts, are getting paid for what they know. When you get paid for what you KNOW, you and your knowledge become irreplaceable and instantly more valuable. You don't see companies as quick to let go decision makers, subject-matter experts, and visionaries. The higher you climb the organizational chart, the less physical/tangible work it appears the bosses do compared to their subordinates, yet they always get paid more. That's because getting paid for what you know always reaps more rewards and profits than getting paid for what you do. The team owner always gets paid more than the players. The surgeons always get paid more than the nurses, who always get paid more than the receptionists, and so on.

Later in the book, I'll break down how to get to what you know and start getting paid for it. That's the entire crux of what becoming a Passionpreneur is all about.

PLEASE DON'T QUIT YOUR DAY JOB ...(YET)!

I told you I would get back to why I stress not quitting your day job. I remember my days in network marketing and how eager I was to quit my full-time job with the telephone company so that I could go full-time in my business. I was making waves in my business and having tremendous success. I did what many others before me had done. I had convinced myself that "If I can make this much part-time, I could make so much more if I were full-time!" So, I quit. Biggest mistake ever.

It was a big mistake for several reasons. A few of which were 1) I hadn't properly prepared myself to go full-time; 2) I hadn't saved enough money to support myself to go full-time; 3) My business wasn't strong enough to support me going full-time. I could go on with why quitting too soon was a mistake (like not having your spouse on board with the decision), but I think you get the picture. The point is don't get things out of order.

Let's take a look at what happens when you do things the right way:

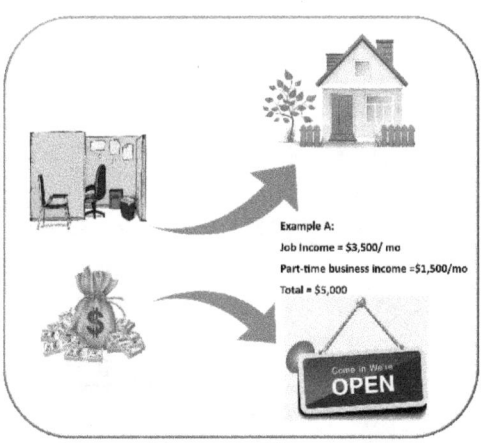

In this example, when you build your passion-driven revenue while keeping your job, your job income continues to go towards your home and family. Your business revenue can then be reinvested into your business to help it grow. For instance, if you're bringing home $3,500 a month from work and bring in an extra $1,500 from your

Passionpreneur business, that's a total of $5,000. Nothing suffers. Home is still taken care of and you are having fun growing a business. You're generating extra income doing something you love instead of getting a second job you'd hate on top of the first one you probably hate.

Here's where too many people (including me) mess up. They see that extra $1,500 coming in and start thinking "If I can make $1,500 with 10 hours, imagine how much I'd make if I were giving that 40 hours a week." They convince themselves that more time commitment is all that's needed to see even more success in their business venture. The reality is here's what happens when you quit your job too soon:

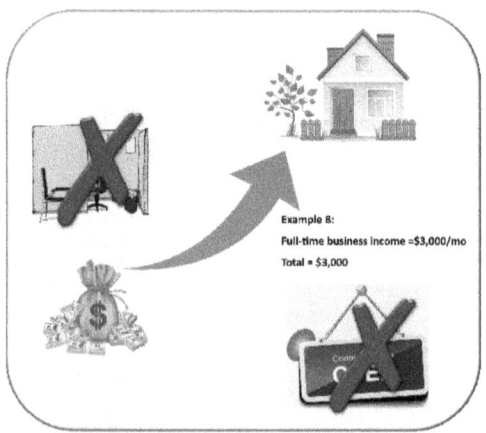

A few things happen when you quit your job too soon. First, you cut off the one secure income stream you had. That $3,500 in our example is gone. Secondly, according to a 2017 GoBanking Rates survey, 57% of Americans have less than $1,000 in savings. So even if you're ten times above average, and have $10,000 in savings, you're probably not financially secure enough to quit your job and go full-time yet. Third, even if you doubled your business income, that puts you at $3,000 a month. That's great for your business, BUT now that money has to go towards home expenses since you quit your job. You can no longer afford to invest in your business, because now that business income must go towards household expenses. You essentially begin strangling your business for cash, until it dies. Once the business income dies, you're forced to find yourself a job again and start from scratch. I've been there. There aren't too many worst feelings than walking with your tail between your legs having to admit you jumped to soon and messed up.

Finally, when you leave your job too soon, the fun leaves as well. The minute you shift your business from supplemental income to primary income, and now you HAVE to get it done versus want to get it done, that introduces a whole new type of stress on every aspect of your business and life. The thing you were once passionate about becomes an albatross around your neck. Your once supportive spouse who was down like four flats for your dream, starts wanting things like food in the fridge, mortgage paid on time, and gas in the tank and you have no idea where the money is coming from. You begin isolating yourself from your friends and family out of shame of your failure and simply not being able to afford to hang out. Look, things will get dark real fast. You can believe me on this one or go out and learn the hard way. Or better yet, you can keep reading and learn about the proper order to build your passion-driven revenue streams.

There are very real benchmarks you should attain in your business before you ever even consider quitting your day job. Let's explore those now.

FIND YOUR PASSION

Benchmark #1 is to find your passion. Obviously, you cannot become a Passionpreneur if you don't even know what your passion is. Fortunately for you, you got started a few pages ago writing out your passion. If you didn't complete that question and write out your passion, I'll give you a minute to go back and do so. No really, go back now and figure out what you're most passionate about. It's kind of important to the rest of the book. I'll wait. Great, now that you've expressed that which you're passionate about, it's time for the next benchmark. You can't just walk off your job because you're passionate about kite making.

MONETIZE IT

Benchmark #2 is finding as many ways to monetize your passion. Having a passion is great, but if we're talking about making a living doing what you love and building passion-driven revenue streams, then we have to know that our passion can be monetized. Take a few minutes now and write out as many ways possible that you can think to monetize your passion. If you cannot come up with at least 30 ways to monetize your passion, you may want to reconsider two things. You may want to reconsider if that's really something you're passionate about, and you may want to reconsider if it is really something that could one day provide a full-time income for you and your family. Get as creative as you can with your list. No idea is a bad idea. The goal is to simply brainstorm as many ideas as possible. We'll sift through them in the next step.

PROVE IT

Benchmark #3 is where we must "show and prove". Once you have selected your methods from Benchmark #2, the next thing to do is go out there and prove that your idea can generate income. (Don't worry about having the answers and methods to do this yet. I'm simply laying out the benchmarks here. Later in the book I'm going to give you the Passionpreneur Roadmap to use to go out and prove it.) This is usually the point where most new entrepreneurs get excited and make that big mistake of leaving their jobs too soon. They've proven their idea can make a little money and they're convinced the only thing holding them back from major success, is the time they're spending at their 9-5.

Don't make that same mistake. Proving your passion can generate income is great if your plan is to create a new job for yourself. If you leap at that prove it phase, you will find yourself always starting from zero every month and stressed about how you are going to make ends meet over the next 30 days. Becoming a Passionpreneur isn't about simply making money, but it's about generating automated passive income that works with or without you. The real freedom and success comes with the next two benchmarks.

DUPLICATE IT

This is where things start getting interesting. You've reached the level of proving your ideas and passions can generate income, but before you consider leaving your job, the next benchmark you must reach is to duplicate your success. What provides more freedom? Being a barber or owning a barber shop and having 10 barbers pay you booth rent? Your next goal is to duplicate your efforts through the work of other people or systems.

As long as you're the only means by which your company makes money, every time you're off, your company is closed. Want to take vacation for a week? How will your company survive if you're the only producer? Don't mess around and get sick or live in an area of inclement weather. You'll find yourself in a financial hardship faster than you can blink. This is one of the biggest selling points in the network marketing industry. Duplication allows you to earn a percentage of the efforts of everyone else in your organization. This isn't a network marketing book, but the principle is just as important in building your Passionpreneur business.

Your goal should be to duplicate your efforts as fast and as many times as possible. That may be by building a team, or it may be through the use of technology, but the sooner you can free yourself from being the sole person responsible for the revenue of your company, the sooner you'll be ready to even consider going full-time.

AUTOMATE IT

The final frontier of becoming a full-time Passionpreneur is automating the processes of your business so that it is on autopilot and works with minimal input from you as possible. This final benchmark is what all seek, but very few ever reach. For most Passionpreneurs, this step isn't going to be one you can accomplish alone (unless your business IS automation). Technology is constantly changing and updating. Innovation is the only constant in automation. Every day there's an easier more efficient way to automate your business and free up your time.

To really transform your business into an automated revenue-generating machine, it will take more in-depth consulting and advice. But for the sake of this list, just know that automation is the holy grail you should seek before walking away from your full-time job. You're not really ready to be in business for yourself full-time until you know that every day your business has systems in place that are capturing leads, walking prospects through your sales funnels, communicating with your customers, doing sales presentations 24/7, and handling all of your back office business activities without you having to lift a finger. When your business has reached that level...

...THEN YOU CAN CONSIDER QUITTING YOUR JOB

So how are you feeling? I know that was a lot of information and groundwork laid in this first section. Are you still excited about becoming a Passionpreneur? It is important we deal with the mindset and get some foundational principles in you before we start getting into the how-tos.

I did a podcast episode on "The Patience For The Process". You can listen to it by subscribing to The Passionpreneur Podcast on iTunes, Spotify, or Google Podcasts. In that episode I talk about why it is so important to respect the process and not try to skip steps. I'm sure this isn't the first business book you've read. I'm sure this isn't your first time trying to figure out how to grow your business. The reason this time will be different, assuming you put in the necessary work, is because I'm giving you the foundation, the bedrock, you need to make sure you have the fortitude and know how to stick to it and persevere.

You've thought about what your passion is, you've taken the Passionpreneur Assessment to see if this is for you, seen where you fit in the Passionpreneur Matrix, you've learned how to build your business upon a solid foundation, how to set S.T.U.P.I.D. goals, the importance of getting paid for what you know, and how to build your business before you mess up and quit your job too soon. The next thing we need to do is light a fire under you. Get you excited about life and about pursuing your passions and dreams again. In the next section we're going to do just that. I'm going to show you how to re-ignite the fire within that the world has tried to permanently extinguish.

RE-IGNITE YOUR FIRE WITHIN

My original concept for this book was for it to be a tool to help people rekindle their passions, reclaim their purpose, and revive their dreams. Knowing how many people are living their day-to-day lives unsatisfied, lead me to seek ways to help people spark that excitement in themselves again. Far too often I see people go to speakers for help to get motivated. I'm not a motivator. I'm a coach. Sure, you may be motivated by things I teach, but there's a huge difference between a motivator and a coach.

The motivator gets on stage and gets you all excited, get you pumped up, gets you cheering and screaming all kinds of mantras. They bring the fire and get you feeling ready to take over the world. They ask, "Do you feel good?!!" And you're like "YES!!!" They ask, "Are you ready to be a winner?!!!" And you yell "YES!!!" You leave and run to your car like "YES!!! This feels great! I'm going to take over the www...what do I do next??"[insert confused face emoji]

There you are sitting in your car, excited about the possibilities of life, but you realize you have no idea what to do. You're left there empty and confused after a little while because all you got was on fire, and it wasn't even your fire. It was the speaker, the motivator, who brought their fire and set you on fire. They were the flame who ignited you. But what happens is, the further you get away from their flame, the harder it is for your flame to stay lit. The more removed you get from the motivator, the dimmer your fire becomes because they were your source. You're excited and motivated, but you have no clue what to do! You weren't given any strategies, or tips or coaching. All you got was a pep rally.

As a coach, what I do, and what I'm doing with _Becoming A Passionpreneur_, is showing you how to re-ignite the fire within YOU. I want to show you how to become the fire for yourself. As your coach, my purpose is to give you the strategies, the tools, and the game plan, but the fire is in you. This process, and specifically this section of the book, is all about re-igniting the fire within YOU. Once you re-ignite your own fire, wherever you go, you will always have the strongest flame. I don't want you getting excited from me and burning off my flame. I can't be with you all the time. If you're counting on me or anyone else to light your fire for you to succeed, you will find yourself in a constant state of starting and stopping, highs and lows, success and failure. But when you re-ignite your own flame, it goes wherever you go. You are always closest to the source when the source is you. This journey is all about re-igniting the fire within you. You know that fire you let die because "life got in the way"? Yeah, that one. That's the fire we're going to re-ignite!

#1 REKINDLE YOUR PASSION

Let's go back to how this concept was birthed and that cashier in the grocery store. I've spoken to tens of thousands of people. Sometimes I've done day-long eight-hour seminars and never once have I midway through a seminar, around noon thought to myself "Man, I can't wait until five o'clock so I can go home." I'm always like "I could do two or three more DAYS at this!" The fact is, once you tap into your passion, once you tap into the thing that you're excited about, that which gives your life meaning and purpose, you find yourself no longer counting hours. When I'm at work and doing what I was created to do, when I'm actively creating, there is no clock in my head. There is no "I can't wait for this to be over." There is no "When do I get off?" Because I'm in my purpose and I'm doing what I was created to do, I never want it to end. My only wish is that more people, especially YOU, understood that you too can feel that!

There's something out there that will make you feel that feeling as well. Maybe you already know what it is but have stopped pursuing it.

Or, maybe you're still searching to find it. Just know it's out there. We get so stuck on- we gotta pay bills, we gotta accumulate "things", we gotta do things that give us some appearance of status that make us look good to other people, over doing what gives us true fulfillment and purpose. We get so caught up in things like "What will people think of me if I'm not making this amount of money, if I'm not holding this title, or driving this car?" That's just silly to me. I just wish that more people understood that true joy and fulfillment comes from going after things you're truly passionate about and purposed to do.

That's what this entire book is about. My focus with *Becoming A Passionpreneur* is to really get you to tap into what it is you were purposed to do, what makes you excited, what you're passionate about, and focusing 100% of your energy into going after THAT. I've spent so much time in my life trying to do the things I felt were "right". I felt I had to do what was right by society's standards, my family and friend's standards and what others felt I should be doing in order to be considered successful. Every time I found myself settling to appease others, I found myself feeling most miserable. It was only those times that I fully pursued my passion that I felt alive, happy and fully available to be used by God.

Sometimes consequences of our past decisions in life catch up with us and force us to make decisions where we must put dreams on the back burner in order to survive the right now. You have to work, and you need income, so you get any job just to take care of your immediate needs. There's not much good that happens when you're broke, so having a steady paycheck is a good thing. Some income is always better than no income at all. But once you get past the point of needing income and transition into a mindset of needing fulfilment, there aren't too many jobs that are designed to give that fulfilment to you.

Think back to when you were in elementary school when you were asked what you want to be when you grew up. What was it that got you excited? What was it that when you were in your room alone you could just do for hours on end? Even today, what is it that you just love to do and can't ever seem to get enough time to dedicate to doing? Those are the things that you need to tap into. That's the foundation of your passion. That fulfilment you get from those things when money isn't even attached to it- that's your passion! Find that thing that gets you excited, gets the blood going and makes you feel alive and DO THAT!

I know you can't just drop everything today and live off your passion. I'm not saying go quit your job today or ever. You may never be able to live off your passion, but that's no excuse not to live a passionate life. You have got to put a life plan in place to go after that thing which you're passionate about. A plan to go and become that person that you were designed and purposed to be.

You must do it! You must find a way! You will never be fully happy and fulfilled until you wake up every morning living a purposeful and passionate life. Stop wasting your life watching the clock and the most exciting thing in your day being quitting time. Rekindle your passion and begin living a life worth living!

#2 RECLAIM YOUR PURPOSE

Somewhere roughly around November 1948, 250 million sperm fought their way along Fallopian Tube Highway towards the town of Conceptionville in the land of Margaret. In this town one pre-destined sperm met and fertilized one pre-destined egg and about 40 weeks later, on August 6, 1949, a girl child, Jaqueline (which means "may God protect"), was born. Jacqueline was no ordinary baby. Jaqueline was born with Sickle Cell Anemia, a debilitating disease of the red blood cells which causes excruciating pain. In 1949 there wasn't much known about ways to treat the disease. Doctors told her parents that Jacqueline would not live past 6 years old.

Fast forward 25 years to January 1975, and that girl Jacqueline who wasn't supposed to live past 6 years old would wind up giving birth to a 10-pound 2-ounce baby boy she and her husband Harry would name, Ryan (which means "Little King). Where Man said he'd give the baby 6 years to live, God said "No, I have a purpose for her life so *I will protect her* until one day she gives birth to a *little king* whose purpose will be even greater." I hope I didn't get too deep right there but man that blessed me!

Here's why that moves me. My entire life I watched my mother fight through her illness and raise me and my sister despite all she went through. We didn't have much in the way of "things", but we always had what we needed. She gave us as rich a childhood as a middle-class single mother could give two kids growing up in the 80's. In January

2000, I turned 25, I got married that May, purchased my first home in June, and then the unthinkable happened. On August 10, 2010, just 4 days after her 51st birthday, my mother Jacqueline suddenly fell ill from complications brought on by her Sickle Cell and passed away.

My entire world came crashing down on that day. Everything I had ever done, every goal I had ever made, was all centered on making HER life easier. My goals were all about finding ways to repay my mother for all the things she had done for my sister and me and now she was gone. Here I was at 25 years old, newly married for just two and a half months, and she was gone. Talk about being lost and completely broken.

In the weeks and months following her death I really began to question what this journey called life was all about. Why did God take my mother away from me so soon? I was just beginning to reach those "adult" milestones and my biggest cheerleader was now gone. One day while in church, God showed me that my mother's purpose in my life specifically, was to birth me and nurture me right up to the point where I was ready and able to begin walking in my own purpose. She *had* to live past 6 years old if for no other reason but to give birth to me and pour those 25 years of nurturing and development into me so that I could fulfill MY purpose!

When I think about how pre-ordained our lives are and how many elements had to be put perfectly into place decades and even centuries before we were born in order for us to be in position to fulfil the plan God has for our lives, there's just no way I can believe we weren't put here with a purpose. A greater purpose than just going to work every day and being one in the countless number. When I look at every twist in turn in my life and every obstacle and challenge I was faced with to make me better, all I can do is humbly thank God for choosing and using me. I know without a doubt I was placed on this Earth at this time to fulfil a grand purpose.

So why are you here? I'm not asking what are you capable of doing (your talents and skills), but why are you HERE (your purpose and destiny)? What is the reason God created YOU and put you on this Earth? That's every person's Million Dollar Question. For some, they discover their answer early on; for others they spend their entire life searching for the answer. If you're unable to give an answer right now to why you're here it isn't the end of the world. As long as you at least accept that there IS an answer and there is a reason you are here, that's the most important thing. We at least have a strong foundation upon which to build. All you have to do is being willing to go on the journey of discovering and accepting that purpose.

If you're reading this book about re-igniting your fire, then it's possible that at some point you became aware of your purpose, but you stopped pursuing it. I've been there! I know my purpose is to reach people through multiple forms of media and empower and entertain them with media with a purpose. I've written bestselling books, I've hosted national radio and television shows, I've spoken to thousands of people across the country, I've created television shows, I've developed DVD programs, I've written songs, I've written blogs. Some would say

I've done a lot! However, even with that resume' there's one other thing I've done- I've QUIT!

I really get into depth in my book *Create A Better YOU!* about my dark period when I quit on my purpose and just wanted to "be normal", but that's what I did. I allowed the cares of life to press me down so hard that I no longer was inspired to fulfill my purpose. The funny thing about purpose though is it doesn't take "No" for an answer very easily. Purpose doesn't let you rest until it is your main pursuit. Purpose will hound your every thought when you try your hardest to ignore it. Eventually, I had a talk with the man in the mirror and decided I would no longer forfeit my purpose and it was time to reclaim it.

Reclaiming your purpose is as simple as making a decision that your purpose will be your only pursuit. Once you accept the call God has placed on your life and yield to Him for direction, a life of purpose will be your most rewarding and fulfilling life. If you've fallen into the trap of forfeiting your purpose or putting it on the back burner, choose today to reclaim your purpose and begin going after it. After all my mother overcame and went through to prepare me for my purpose, how could I walk away and quit? Look at all that's been done to prepare you for a moment like this in your life and ask yourself the same question. Stop running and reclaim your purpose! Someone 100 years from now is counting on you!

#3 REVIVE YOUR DREAMS

If you look at the cover of this book, in the bottom right corner you'll see a heart monitor reading with a heart in it. When I talk about re-igniting your fire, this is what I'm talking about. Our dreams are those things that get our heart beating and make us feel alive. Think back to when you were a kid and what you dreamed of back then. Think about all the things you said you wanted to become, before you let fear, doubt and bills creep in.

We have all been there. I keep harping to that 70% of disengaged American employees. Can you imagine if all of them dusted off their dreams and began pursuing them today? Can you imagine how much more joy they'd feel in life? What was your dream? Why did you give up on it? Are you ready to revive it? It's never too late.

I recently had my 25th high school reunion so I was going through my old senior memory book. I got to the page where it asked what we wanted to be when we grew up. To my surprise, even back in 12th grade, my dream was to be an entrepreneur. All my life, all I've ever wanted to do was to own and run my own business. At that time, I didn't know what type of business I wanted, but I just knew my dream was to be my own boss.

Along the way I faced many challenges and doubters, but my dream never left me. I went through ups and downs, feast and famine, joy and pain, but through it all, GreeneHouse Media is here and still growing. I'm living my dream every day. I know the joy it brings me and I want to see so many others experience that same joy and fulfillment from the work they do. I always say, "Dreams are man-made, purpose is God-made, Destiny is where the two of them meet." God has a purpose for you that lines up with your dreams. He hasn't given up on your purpose, so you can't give up on your dreams.

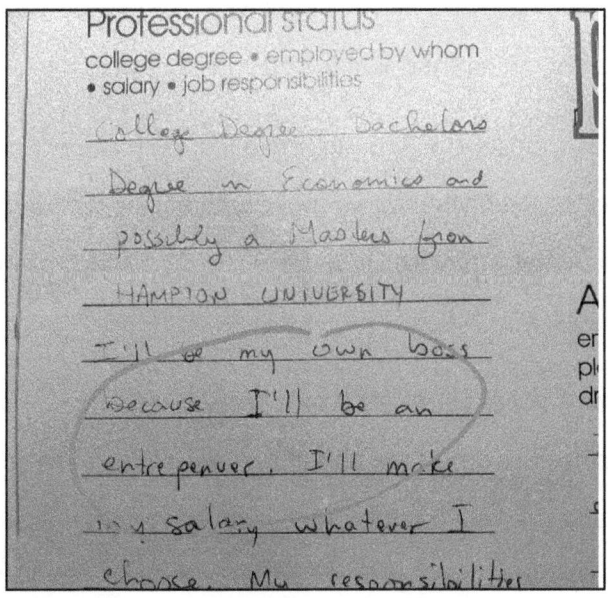

#4 RE-VISIT YOUR WHY

This is my 6th solo book I've authored. I've been a contributing writer for three others. In every one of my solo books, I talk about knowing your WHY. Guess what. I'm going to talk about it again in this book. Your WHY is just that important. When we are talking about re-igniting your fire, one important place to start is re-visiting your WHY. Sometimes we allow the tests of life to knock us off course and we lose track of why we're pressing toward our goals in the first place.

Your WHY should have four components to it. 1) it should motivate you; 2) someone or something other than yourself should be at the center of your WHY; 3) it must be strong enough to make you cry; and 4) you must be willing to die for it. If you've quit on your WHY and you can live comfortably with that, then your WHY wasn't strong enough to begin with. Your commitment to your WHY should be so strong that death is the only thing that would stop you from pursing it.

Orlando Bishop is the founder of Align Performance, a personal performance coaching practice. I spoke with him about how he got into business and what motivates him. Here's what he had to say about his WHY.

"The idea of doing work "for a paycheck" drains me. I've done it. We do what we need to do. At the end of the day, though, it's not the way I want to spend my life. The idea that I can earn money to help people live happier, healthier lives gets me out of bed in the morning. I got into coaching through being coached. At a low point in my life, personally and professionally, a friend who was moving into executive coaching offered me free coaching. She could get some practice and I could get some help. So, I accepted. A few sessions in I said, "Pam, I think I can do what you're doing." Everything changed from there."

If you want an in-depth training on how to develop a strong WHY, I'd encourage you to pickup my first book <u>Success Is In Your Hand</u> where I spend an entire chapter teaching on how to develop your strong WHY. For the sake of this book, and not teaching the same thing a 6th time, I won't get into how to do it. Just know it's important to always re-visit your WHY and make sure it still moves you.

#5 RE-IMAGINE YOUR LIFE AS SUCCESSFUL

What would your life look like if you had all the success you seek? Now, had I asked you to imagine what you would do if you won the Powerball, I bet you'd run off an entire well thought out fantasy. Something that you have a 1 in 350,000,000 chance of experiencing, and you already know what kind of mansion you would buy, which private island you're moving to, and the color of your space shuttle you're buying. But when asked to imagine what success looks like to you- you get all shy and insecure.

Speaking for myself, when I was going through my darkest period between 2009-2013 and I had quit on business and my purpose, I had conceded that my life would just be a normal average existence. After my divorce, I had zero motivation and drive. I was ready to find a regular ol' job and live a regular ol' life. But purpose won't let you run forever. Purpose is like your crazy ex that stalks you everywhere you go until you take them back. No matter how much I tried to give up, my purpose kept calling me like "Whatchu doing?"

It took me re-imagining my life and looking at it from the lens of "How would my life be if I achieved my goals and was successful?" The more I imagined myself as successful, the more I liked the way that life looked. Eventually, I stopped dreaming and started doing. My fire was re-ignited from the possibilities of what was still in store for me. From that point things started to turn around. I met a lovely young lady who I eventually married, and I got back to work on becoming what I was purposed to be. I want you to stop sulking in the doldrums of your current situation and begin to re-imagine yourself as successful. Let that motivate you towards action to become that.

#6 RE-ALIGN YOURSELF WITH BETTER PEOPLE

Here's a truth most people who are unhappy with life never want to hear, "Your circle of people in your life suck." Hold on! Don't throw the book across the room yet. Let me explain. When I say your circle sucks, it doesn't mean they don't love you or that they aren't totally awesome people. What I mean is, if your fire has been out for any length of time, and those closest to you haven't noticed or attempted to help you re-ignite your fire, then they suck at that area of your life.

People are your most valuable resource. If you have a dream to achieve anything significant, you are going to need people to help. If your circle of friends and family aren't pushing you toward your goals or cannot support you how you need, then you need to consider realigning yourself with different networks of people.

If you light one match in the book of matches while it's still in the book, every other match in the book will catch on fire. The other matches can't help but to catch on fire due to their proximity to the lit match. If you need to re-ignite your fire, you need to find people who can be that lit match to you. If you start aligning yourself with goal getters and ambitious people, you will either do one of two things.

Either you're going to leave them, or you're going to join them and awaken your ambitions too. I know your mama always warned you about the company you keep. It's time to listen to her and find you some new friends.

#7 REBEL AGAINST THE RULES AND NORMS

There's a saying that goes, "I would rather ask for forgiveness than permission." Man, I live by that! When it comes to adhering to rules and norms, I am like that 5-year old kid who won't stop asking "But, why?" The quickest way to get me to rebel against conformity is by telling me "that's how we do it, because that's how it's always been done."

There's an old African parable about 5 caged monkeys. Actually, I don't know where the parable came from. It may be from Argentina or Arizona, but for this book, the parable came from Africa. Anyway, the parable goes as such. There were five monkeys in a cage, whenever one monkey would climb to the top of the cage to escape, the handler would spray all the monkeys with water. No matter what, anytime a monkey climbed to the top, the monkeys would be sprayed with water.

Eventually, the handler removed one monkey and replaced it with a monkey that had never been sprayed with the water. As soon as that monkey tried to escape, the other four monkeys attacked it and pulled it down so they wouldn't be sprayed. Because the monkeys pulled the other one down, the handler didn't spray them. One by one, the handler replaced each of the original monkeys until finally there were five new monkeys who had never been sprayed by the water. When the fifth monkey was introduced to the cage, it tried to escape and the other four attacked it and pulled it down. Those five monkeys never tried to escape the cage again.

Here's the thing, at that point, none of the monkeys could tell each other why they were pulling the others down. None of them had ever been sprayed by the water. They were all fighting each other from escaping, solely because that's just what had always been done to them. How many times have you found yourself following rules or adhering to norms that no one can explain *why* that's how things are done? Sometimes breaking the rules and daring to blaze a new path is exactly what you need to re-ignite your fire within.

Rules and norms aren't designed to foster creativity and greatness. The exact opposite is true. All our lives we've been taught coloring inside the lines was the only way to do it. If that were true, then why are artists like Basquiat and Picasso revered as such geniuses? I don't think they've ever seen a line they colored within. Genius occurs outside the lines. Greatness lives outside the norms. Don't be afraid to take risks just because something has always been done one way.

#8 RECOGNIZE NEW OPPORTUNITIES

Sometimes we get caught trying to fit a square peg into a round hole. Sometimes what we are trying just doesn't work or it wasn't meant to work for us. Instead of beating your head against a wall trying to make it work, take time to explore new opportunities that may be best suited for you. Other times, maybe we were operating in the right place and had success but got burned out or bored. Because you succeeded in one area, doesn't mean that's all you can do for the rest of your life.

I interviewed Purse Paparazzi Founder and Chief Fashion Officer, Quinn Conyers about her entrepreneurial journey. Purse Paparazzi creates custom purses for women who are members of sororities or attended a historically black college or university (HBCU). Quinn sells purses, but her true passion is in public speaking. Here's what she had to say about how she used her purse business to create new opportunities for her speaking career.

"I love my bag business, but speaking is really my passion! I ended up using public speaking to really boost my business! I incorporated speaking into my business as an income stream, marketing strategy and funding source. I truly enjoy hosting workshops and serving as a speaker at events to help other entrepreneurs speak about their business with courage and confidence."

Look at how recognizing new opportunities opened doors for Quinn. When she faced funding shortages, she again sought opportunities to overcome rather than quit.

"My biggest challenge was money for inventory! I ended up pre-selling to fulfill orders and pitching my business in pitch competitions and winning over $34,000 in funding. Another challenge I had was staying resilient after rejection. It's hard to keep pushing when sales or slow. I kept pressing by trying different marketing strategies, getting

insight from mentors and really understanding "no", setbacks, and obstacles are a part of the journey."

If you're getting frustrated or burned out, take time to recognize what new opportunities are out there for you to take advantage of.

#9 RE-CHARGE YOUR BATTERY BY HAVING FUN

No dream is worth chasing if you can' have fun doing it. I am notoriously a workaholic. My wife can attest to the fact that sometimes, I am so focused on work, that I will go all day and forget to eat. It is very difficult for me to sit still and do nothing. My mind is always on, always thinking about the next project. As a creative, in my mind I am always creating something new or improving upon something. It's very rare you will ever find me not thinking.

Since I work in my passion, my work doesn't feel like work. So, vacations never feel necessary because I never feel stressed about work. I love what I do. BUT, vacation and mental breaks are so vital to your health and even your business. Taking time away allows you to recharge and re-center your mind. Sometimes the best thing for your work, is to take a break and have some fun.

All work and no play sounds good on a t-shirt, but that died with the 80's. Mental health and wellness, as well as your physical health are just as important as the profits and losses on your income statements. If you are stuck trying to re-ignite your fire, channel your inner Stella and go get your groove back! (I fully understand that if you are under 35 years old, you may have to Google that reference to understand, but I'm sticking with it. #GenX). The point is let your hair down and go have some fun. Life is stressful even without trying to start a business. Plan yourself a quick weekend getaway and re-charge.

#10 REMEMBER THAT YOU ARE CHOSEN

Finally, I will give you this. I don't believe in chance or coincidence. We are all intelligently designed by God for a destiny He wants us to fulfill. You are chosen by Him to succeed at what he called you to do and become. If you give up on your purpose, you are giving up on Him and everything He called you to be.

I know the road gets tough and often times quitting feels like the best option. As human beings, we are all going to quit at some point. The thing that makes your great, is how fast you get back up and how much stronger you are when you come back. My favorite scripture is Mark 10: 29-31:

"Truly I tell you," Jesus replied, "no one who has left home or brothers or sisters or mother or father or children or fields for me and the gospel will fail to receive a hundred times as much in this present age: homes, brothers, sisters, mothers, children and fields—along with persecutions—and in the age to come eternal life. But many who are first will be last, and the last first."

God promised if you dedicate your work to Him and stand on His word, He will bless you one hundred times over, now in this time.

Weeping may endure for a night, but joy comes in the morning. God has chosen you and He will never leave nor forsake you. Your only job is to get up when you fall, fight back when you're hit, and never forget whose you are. You are chosen. Walk in your blessing.

9 BUSINESS MYTHS THAT ARE KEEPING YOU BROKE

To this point we have tackled the mindset needed to become a Passionpreneur and we've discussed several ways to re-ignite your fire within. Now as we get into the principles of building passion-driven revenue streams, it is important we tackle some business myths you may or may not have dealt with on your journey. Many of these myths are schools of thought that sound like good advice at face value, but when you really dive deeper, they tend to be more harmful than they are helpful.

As we go through these business myths it is important that you begin shifting how you look at business. Your ideas of what business leadership and successful entrepreneurship look like to this point may have been biased by certain beliefs you held or lessons you learned along the way that have been costing you more money than they've been making you.

MYTH #1: YOU EARNED IT SO YOU DESERVE TO SPEND IT

Have you ever said this to yourself? Have you ever lied to yourself and said, "I worked hard for this so I'm going treat myself"? Here's why this is a myth that's keeping you broke. Typically, this mindset is used to justify making some purchase that isn't business related. It's typically a luxury item you're splurging on that you know you shouldn't be throwing away money on, but you use your business success as justification for "rewarding" your success and spending that profits you made. Just because you earn revenue doesn't mean you *deserve* to spend it. Your business deserves that money, not you.

This doesn't mean you'll never buy yourself anything nice, but your focus can't be on buying *things*. You will never become financially successful by letting every dollar that comes in, go out to fund someone else's dream because you are a victim of materialism. Your business won't grow if you are constantly spending all your profit instead of reinvesting it into your business. Get that myth out of your mind. Take that money and build your passion-driven revenue streams.

I tell ladies all the time, if you don't have enough money to put inside the purse what you paid for the purse, then you don't deserve to purse. Fellas, same thing. How is it that every shirt you wear has to be Ralph Lauren Polo and you can't even afford to play real polo? We're building businesses here, not Christmas slush funds. It's not about how much money you make, it's about how much you keep.

MYTH #2: YOUR JOB IS ENOUGH

I want to remind you before I go further here about the earlier lesson in the book about quitting your job. There's a process you must go through to prove yourself ready before quitting your job and becoming a full-time Passionpreneur. I'm not telling you to go leave your job. What I do want you to understand here is that your job isn't going to be enough. If your plan is to live a modest life, retire one day and live worry-free, the stark reality is your job is not enough. The main reason it's not enough is because you don't control it. On any day you could be out of work through no fault of your own.

As we've seen in recent years, even a "good gub'mint job" isn't so good and secure anymore. If all your eggs are in your one job basket, the day they lay you off or furlough you is a terrible time to find out your basket had a hole in it and all your eggs fell. Now you *and* your eggs are broke.

Think about your dream lifestyle. I want you go ahead, take a second right now. Think about the lifestyle you'd live if money weren't an issue. You have that in your mind? Where are you? What are you wearing?

What kind of car are you driving? Money's not an issue. This is your dream. What does your house look like? Is it a big house? Is it a log cabin? Is it a tiny home? Where are you going for vacation? How long are you staying?

Now here's the question. Who at your job, who currently does what you do, lives your dream? Who's living the lifestyle you dream of at your job? Anyone? That's why your job isn't enough. It doesn't mean leave it, but it just means you must find other ways to supplement and build. You must find other ways to grow your finances outside of your job if those are the things that you really dream of having. I believe for Passionpreneurs, your job should be your steppingstone, not your bedrock.

MYTH #3: THIS IS AS GOOD AS IT GETS

This one here is a double-sided myth. I call it that because "this is as good as it gets" can come from both directions. You could be in a position where you feel like you made it and accomplished all you were out to accomplish and believe "this is as good as it gets". Conversely, you could be unfulfilled and upset feeling as if your work is in vain and there's nothing else out there for you. That feeling of hopelessness could also lead you to believe more negatively that "this is as good as it gets".

Complacency is the enemy of excellence. Read that again. Complacency is the enemy of excellence. What do I mean by that? I define excellence as "when good enough is never good enough". When you get to a position of believing this is as good as it gets, what you're essentially saying is "this is as hard as I'm willing to work." You're saying you're not working any harder to move past this point. If you are sitting on top and ready to take your feet off the gas, I would encourage you find more people to help, teach and uplift. There's always someone else out there looking for what you offer. If you're on the bottom and you're frustrated by everyone else around you who is having success and you think, the bottom is just where you belong and it doesn't get any better than that, I've called my man Maury, and the test results prove- that's a lie!

If you're honest with yourself, the truth is you probably just haven't put in enough work. You must work more to get more. At some point you let distractions come along cloud your vision. You let other people get in your ear and tell you this is all you deserve. They said you weren't made to be an entrepreneur and you believed them. They told you "it doesn't take all that" to be happy, so you gave up on your dreams. You started qualifying your dreams with statements like "I don't even need the whole thing, just give me a piece" and saying stuff like "This is cool. It's better than nothing." But if you know you have greater things waiting for you, if you just do the work to get there? Why wouldn't you? Good enough is never good enough.

MYTH #4: THE MONEY IS IN THE LIST

This myth is kind of tricky because people believe the money is in the list. You will hear that in sales training is all the time. "Build your list!"

Building your prospects list is important, vital even to your business success, but the money isn't *in* the list. The money is in having the systems and knowledge that allow you to exploit and monetize the list for maximum revenue. Whether you have an email list of 100 subscribers, 2,500 subscribers, or 30,000 subscribers, if you don't have any way to control the flow of information to your list and generate revenue from that list, all you have is a bunch of stranger's names.

Let me share an example. I am a publisher. I write books. In the past I have also published other authors' books. Now, I help authors market and sell their books through my company, Indie Author PRO. (If you're interested in getting coaching on writing or marketing your book, visit www.indiauthorpro.com for info on that.) If you are an aspiring author or know someone who desires to publish a book, here's what happens. An author writes a book on their own and self publishes. Where is the first place they go when they want to sell their book? Amazon.com, right? It's the largest book seller in the world. What happens is, to sell your book on Amazon, Amazon will buy your book at a 40% discount, paying you 60% of your book retail price. If you want to sell your book for $20, Amazon will pay you $12 for the book. Many times, they will sell author's books for less than the author would sell it themselves. But what author is going to walk away from listing their books with the world's largest and most recognized book retailer?

Here's the billion-dollar question. Why is Amazon selling books? Your first response may be that they want to make money. That's true. Amazon makes a LOT of money selling books. But dig a little deeper.

How did they become the world's largest online retailer? Amazon doesn't even create a product. The simply distribute other people's products. How are they able to make so much money? What is Amazon really getting? What they have is the INFORMATION. They know who bought your book, and you don't. They know what else those buyers purchased, and you don't. They know every buying behavior of the purchaser, and you don't. They have the power to say, "Hey, you may like to buy this book since you bought that book.", and you don't.

I've been in publishing for almost 15 years. I still cannot tell you the name of two people who've purchased my books on Amazon because I don't have access to that list and information. Amazon understands the power is not just in having the list, but in knowing how to exploit the information in the list and use it to market effectively. The reality is, Amazon is an information company disguised as an online retailer. Their real business is gathering information about consumer buying behaviors. I won't event get into all the information Amazon gained about citizens and consumers from all the cities who were begging to get them to move their second headquarters to their city.

As a budding Passionpreneur, your goal is two-fold. You want to grow your list of prospects, but you also want to ensure you have systems in place to help maximize the value of your list. You want to know what information your lists give you and how to interpret that information to build more successful communication, marketing, and product offers. The difference between Amazon and almost every independent business around is, when Amazon looks for sponsors, they can provide companies with precise analytics on what consumers they have access to want. Most independent companies simply have a list of strangers who they hope pay attention to their emails.

MYTH #5: IF IT'S GONNA GET DONE RIGHT, YOU HAVE TO DO IT

If you have ever said, "If it's going to get done right, I have to do it", here's the problem with that mindset. If you are always the one doing it, then you are always going to be solopreneur. You are always going to be the one whose business owns you. The goal of becoming a Passionpreneur is to build passion-driven revenue streams we can automate and remove ourselves from the work.

Let's look at it like this. I want you to take a minute right now and think in your head, if you had to put a dollar sign on your worth per hour, what would it be? If you had to say, "I'm worth this amount of money per hour and if you want to hire me, you have to pay me this much", what would that number be? Really think about it and be honest with yourself. Most of us aren't going to be worth $15,000 an hour. Would be nice, but if you were, you probably wouldn't need this book. So, what is a realistic number?

For this example, let's use $500/hr. Let's say $500 is your price tag for an hour of your time. Whether it's a consultation, a speech, tax preparation, cooking, whatever you do, one hour of you doing that thing, could bring in $500. Now, let's look at what it would cost you to hire a professional to create and schedule an email campaign for you.

What would you pay them? Probably $100 an hour, right? Even if it took them five hours to complete the task, wouldn't it be worth it to pay someone else the $500 for five hours, when it would cost you $2,500 to commit those same five hours to writing emails yourself? Do you see now how every time you take on the mindset that you're the only one who can do it right and go do a task yourself that someone else could have done, you're actually losing money by taking yourself out of the real business you should be earning $500/hr to do?

You're essentially costing your business $500/hr any time you're doing work you could have hired someone at $100/hr to do. Anytime you don't *know* how to do something, don't have the *time* to do it, don't *want* to do it, or it doesn't make sense *financially* for you to do it, you need to hire someone else to do it. The only way you're going to grow your business is when you start to release your grip on things. You must let other people in to take care of those parts of your business that are pulling you away from doing the things you're in business to do.

I know in the beginning it may be tough to convince yourself to shell out money to hire professional help, but in the long run it always pays off. The "I gotta do it myself" way of thinking is for corporate managers afraid of empowering their employees for fear they may look better than the boss. In the business world, "help" is not a bad word. The more help you get, the faster and bigger you grow. I challenge you to start by choosing just one aspect of your business to outsource. Start there and gradually work up to the second and third. Watch what a difference it makes.

MYTH #6: NO ONE IS GOING TO PAY YOU THAT MUCH MONEY

This one is a big one. This is one that keep so many entrepreneurs broke. Humans are born with two fears. Fear #1 is the fear of loud noises. Fear #2 is the fear of falling. That's it. Every other fear that we have in our lives, we have learned somewhere throughout our lives. We weren't born with any other fear other than loud noises and falling. So, why do people feel like they aren't worth that amount of money they want to demand? Because they have a fear of asking for what they're worth. Somewhere along the way, they learned to be afraid of demanding their worth.

You may want to charge $3,000 to speak somewhere, but you're afraid the company will say, "No, we'll go find someone else." So, you say you'll do it for free because they told you it will be good exposure. Let me tell you something, I stopped speaking for exposure a long time ago. Truth is, when I call my bills and say, "Hey, I'm going to send you exposure to pay my cell bill this month", they're hanging up on me. I'm like, "Hello? Can you hear me now?" It doesn't work. I want you to understand that it's not that people won't pay you. The problem is you're just too afraid to ask for it. You don't believe in your own value enough to ask for and demand that value.

Stop short-changing your value to the marketplace. Make your price, your price. State it firmly and don't waiver just because the potential client balks initially. When you charge what you want to charge and give people the opportunity to pay it, they will.

I'll give you a secret because I've been there. I'm a speaker, so I'll use speaking as an example. You will agree to speak for free at an event for *exposure*. You'll go and do your talk, and if you're good, you'll crush it. You'll go out there and you'll rock out. The audience will love you. Attendees will flock to your table after your talk and tell you how much they loved your presentation. You can just feel the exposure beginning to pay off with future paid engagements!

Then on your way home you'll find yourself sitting in the car angry at the event organizer because you didn't get paid. You didn't sell enough product so you're mad about that too. They didn't even give you lunch. You had to go and find something to eat on your own after you spent all that gas money driving out there. A few days later, your phone rings and you just know it's Exposure on the other end. Turns out it's the event organizer calling to say everyone loved you so much they'd love for you to come and speak for two more events for FREE.

Now you feel angry AND disrespected, but you're mad at all the wrong people. The only person you should be angry with is yourself for accepting the free gig in the first place when you thought you were worth more. You sold yourself for free. You just gave away your value for free. Don't get angry with the buyer because you sold your talents for the low. No more being afraid of asking for what you're worth. If you're afraid to give it to yourself, let me give you the permission today to go out there and charge what you're worth. It will make you enjoy your business so much more and you're worth it!

MYTH #7: FAKE IT 'TIL YOU MAKE IT

Who hasn't heard this seemingly fun and harmless saying? I remember when I was building my network marketing company, this was one of the more popular mantras. I swear there was someone every week, in every training, encouraging all of us to "fake it 'til we make it". To be clear, they weren't encouraging us to lie or be deceitful about our achievements. They were telling us to act and look as if we'd already achieved the levels of success to which we aspired. It was more so about carrying yourself like the success you wanted to be.

You may be thinking "Ryan, what's so wrong with that?" It's not that there's anything "wrong" with the idea of faking it to you make it, but the consequences of doing so could be detrimental to your success if you're not careful. Faking it and acting as if you have already achieved levels of success that you have not, usually only ends up fooling one person- you. Everyone else knows you're faking it. They all know you're putting on airs to appear to be something you're not. The moment you lose your authenticity in business, you may as well close shop. People only do business with businesses they trust.

What tends to happen is, you've spent so much time *faking* your success, that you forget about actually *making* your success. You forget that you're not the success you portray yourself to be, so you begin neglecting your own growth. You've gone and purchased the designer suits and French-cuff shirts, or the Christian Louboutin heels and designer handbags to look like the person you dream of becoming, but you never invest in personal development workshops and conferences that will help you grow into that person. Instead of focusing on being the student and finding mentors and coaches who could sow into your development, you end up trying to be the teacher.

While faking it 'til you make it, isn't said with negative intentions, the practice could lead to an unconscious derailing of your success. Instead of faking it, admit you need assistance and training to get to where you seek to go. Find all the resources available to help you get there and take advantage. Never be ashamed to be a student. Never be too prideful to seek help. It's time to stop faking it, and just start making it!

MYTH #8: MINDSET IS ALL YOU NEED TO SUCCEED

Here's another myth that trips people up all the time. I teach a lot about mindset. We started this process of becoming a Passionpreneur by first discussing mindset. The right mindset is a cornerstone for achieving any type of success. The problem comes along when people think mindset is all you need. Mindset is not the end all be all to success. All those "think it and achieve it" gurus who convince people that they just have to shift their thinking and they will achieve all the success they've ever imagined, are selling you a gallon-sized jar of snake oil.

Just as the Bible says in James 2:17, "faith by itself, if it does not have works, is dead", mindset without works, is also dead. What good to your success is a positive, properly calibrated mindset, if you don't get off your butt and do the work to succeed? Too often, aspiring entrepreneurs treat their business just how people treat church. In church on Sunday, everyone is excited and dancing and praising, and rejoicing in The Lord. They're ready to wash their sins away (again) and go into the week on fire for Jesus and win next week's "Saint of the Week Award" for being such a great disciple. Then on the way home from church, someone cuts them off in traffic, and before they even got the taste of the communion wine out their mouth, they done cursed out the other driver!

When was the last time you read a great business book, attended an impactful conference, or watched a powerful business webinar, that you were convinced was the missing piece to changing your life and your business? You were on fire and excited about all the new ideas you were ready to unleash on the world thanks to the new information you learned. You told yourself this time was different, and you were ready to finally "do this". Then, the very next day, new mindset and all, you went right back to life as usual. We've all been there. I've done it more times than I care to admit. Understand this: MINDSET − ACTION = FAILURE every time. Mindset is a cornerstone to success, but it's not the key to success. Your unrelenting action, directed by your mindset, is what will guide you to success.

I have two children. God blessed me with an awesome son and a most lovely daughter. At the time of writing this book, my son is 17 years old. As a younger child, he loved building Lego sets. He could put together those huge sets in record time. After he built what was designed to be built, he'd then begin creating his own designs. Some of the most magnificent Lego creations a parent has ever seen were built by my young son. Naturally, every adult started telling him, "Jordan, you're going to grow up to be an engineer." After years of being told that, whenever asked what he wanted to be when he grew up, my son would say he wanted to be an engineer. The only problem was, while he may have had the mindset to become an engineer, he never paired the mindset with the actions necessary to become an engineer.

I could see early on, while he was definitely intelligent enough to become an engineer, he had zero desire to do the work necessary to pursue that path. I eventually encouraged him to seek his true passion and stop telling people he wanted to be an engineer simply because that's what people told him he should be. He discovered theater once he got to high school and found a passion for sound design. He now desires to be a professional foley artist. I know you're asking, "Ryan, what the heck is a foley artist?!" I had the same question. Thanks to my friends at Google, I learned "foley artist" is a fancy name for the person who creates sound for films. Pretty cool, huh?

Now he's clear on what he's passionate about doing and has his mind set on becoming that. Unfortunately, we're still waiting for that action towards the goal to begin. What, you thought this was some ABC Afternoon Special and I was going to say he's more focused than ever and finally doing the work to be all he can be? Nah, this is real life! Real parenting! I told you he's a 17-year old boy. Lazy is his middle name. He and I are still arguing every day about him not applying himself and pursuing his passion wholeheartedly. To be continued...

MYTH #9: IF YOU SHARE YOUR DREAMS WITH OTHERS, SOMEONE WILL STEAL IT

ASPIRING AUTHOR: I have a great idea for a book

ME, THE PUBLISHER: Great, what's the book about?

ASPIRING AUTHOR: It's a book about [insert any book idea here].

ME, THE PUBLISHER: Sounds interesting. What's the title?

ASPIRING AUTHOR: I can't tell you. I don't want you to steal it.

ME, THE PUBLISHER: *befuddled facepalm*

When I was actively publishing books for other authors, I'd have that conversation at least once a month. Even now as an author marketing coach, authors still trust me enough to coach them, but sometimes get apprehensive about sharing their ideas for fear that sharing their ideas would lead to said idea being stolen. As if stealing author's ideas and titles is a solid business model. The truth is, while it's possible your idea could be stolen by someone you shared it with, the likelihood of it happening are so low, the fear is more irrational than realistic.

It's kind of like how Apple has convinced iPhone users their phones are more secure from cyber-attacks and viruses, yet no iPhone user can tell you a single Android phone user whose phone has ever been hacked or stricken with a virus. The truth is, both phones are equally secure.

The enhanced security of an iPhone is a myth. Much like thinking someone is going to take your idea is too.

When I say it's a myth to believe someone is preying on you to steal your ideas, what I mean is, the benefits of sharing your ideas with the right people, far outweigh the chances of someone taking your idea. I hear of people all the time who have ideas in their head they refuse to share with others and those ideas never come to fruition. We live in a time and age where collaboration and synergy make things move at lightning speed. While you are holding your precious idea close to the vest refusing to seek input or help, others are out here telling anyone who will listen about their ideas and getting their projects funded and produced.

How can your idea change the world and your life and legacy, if you refuse to share it with anyone? I still remember when I met with a friend of mine to discuss a business project. I was there to discuss a book I was working on. He is also an author so all during lunch, we were discussing our book projects. Right before we left, he asked me what else was I working on. I somewhat reluctantly mentioned my idea to film a fitness series for kids. I was reluctant to mention it not because I thought he'd take the idea, but because the idea had been on the back burner for so long and I didn't think it was worth discussing. Turns out that after a few more questions, he asked me if he could fund that project. Just like that! A project I had tabled in my mind was now about to get funded and brought to life. All because I shared the idea. Had I kept the idea to myself, FitLife Kids DVD would still be just a dream.

As an aspiring Passionpreneur, you must shift from a scarcity mindset to an abundance mindset. What God has for you, is for you. If He gave you the idea, He'll give you the people to bring forth the idea. As the cliché goes, "Teamwork makes the dream work." Stop keeping everything to yourself and start building yourself some teams of folks who can bring your dreams to life.

DEATH TO ALL SACRED COWS

I read a book years ago by David Bernstein called <u>Death to All Sacred Cows: How Successful Businesses Put the Old Rules Out to Pasture.</u> You can still get the book in Kindle version on Amazon. If you're still struggling with getting past business myths and conventional ways of thinking, his book will give you the push you need. The premise of the book is that corporate America, and by proxy, small business, is ruled by these outdated norms that don't work. His book is an attempt to kill those norms and help create independent creative thought. It's a way to stop doing things just because that's the way they've always been done. It forces you to always ask "But WHY are we doing this and why are we doing it this way?"

That's what breaking free of these business myths is all about. You have the power to do things differently if you'll only be brave enough to go against the grain and risk a bit of discomfort while others look at you like you're crazy. If you've been doing things the safe way all this time and not getting the results you seek, maybe it's because you've been falling for these business myths for too long.

BECOMING A PASSIONPRENEUR

Here is where we really get to work. If you've stuck with me this long, then I know you are serious about re-igniting your fire within and making a living doing what you love. I know you are ready to start building passion-driven revenue streams. This section is all about the Seven Secrets to Creating Passion-Driven Revenue Streams and how to navigate your personalized Passionpreneur Pyramid.

As we go through this section, there will be space provided for you to take notes and begin to hash out just what your vehicle will be and what becoming a Passionpreneur looks like for you specifically. I have also designed a Passionpreneur Pyramid available for free download that you can use for your final draft. It's a little fancier and easier to take with you. You can download it for free at bit.ly/BAPPyramid

I said it was free! What are you waiting for? Go ahead and download the pyramid. Huh? Oh, you can't get to it right now? Fine, well here's what it looks like. But, believe me, you're going to want to download the full-sized color version. Anyway, let's get to Secret #1.

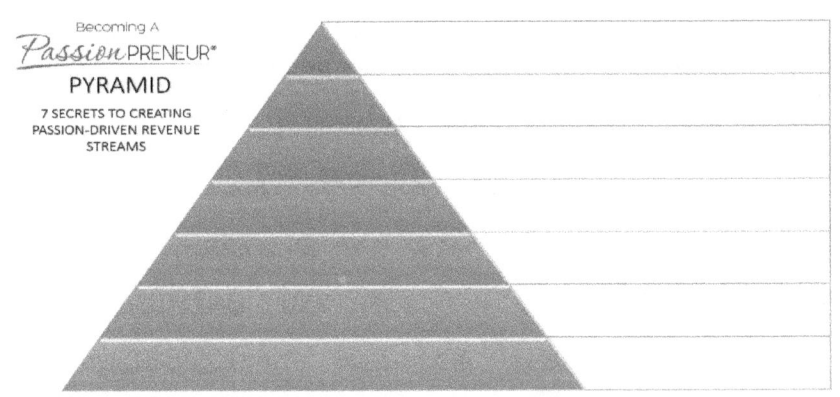

SECRET #1: FIGURE OUT WHAT YOU KNOW

Secret number one is to get paid for what you know, not for what you do. What does that mean? The person who gets paid for what they do will always get paid less than the person getting paid for what they know. Look at any corporation or organization. Who gets paid more? The people at the bottom who are usually the do-ers? Or the people at the top in the offices who are usually the know-ers? Whenever you get paid for what you do, you can easily be replaced by someone or some machine, that can do it better and faster. Knowledge, however, is much more difficult to replace.

Let me give you an example. Let's go back to me building websites. Remember, I don't like building websites, but I can build websites. If I were to build a website for someone else, I could charge them $1,000. That's very cheap, but for the sake of easy math, we'll use $1,000 to build a small website. You may be thinking "$1,000 is good money!" And it is. But what must happen anytime I want another $1,000? I must go and build another website. Every time I want to earn that $1,000, I must go and DO another website.

The goal is to shift from getting paid for what I do to getting paid for what I know. I'm sure there are people out there who would love to learn how to build websites. What if I then go in to the mode of teaching other people how to build websites and teaching them what I KNOW about building websites and transferring that knowledge to them. I could charge $5,000 for that kind of information. I can go from building a website and making $1,000, to teaching people how to build websites for $5,000. I would have to build 5 websites myself just to equal that one $5,000 for that one lesson I taught to that one student. Is it beginning to make sense yet?

The next question to ask is "How do I remove my labor completely from the equation?" If I am teaching the lesson, even though I'm getting $5,000 every time I teach what I know, I still have to go out and DO every lesson. So how do we remove our labor? I'm so glad you asked. What if I recorded that lesson one time and now everyone who wants that lesson registers for my digital academy and watches the same videos I already made? Now I can earn $5,000 every time someone takes the class that I only taught one time. We've gone from building websites for $1,000 (doing), to generating a self-sufficient digital academy (knowing) that generates five times the revenue without us even having to teach the course every time. That's how we fully shift to getting paid for what we know while also removing our labor from the equation.

This is the beginning of generating passion-driven revenue streams and where we will start on your Becoming A Passionpreneur Pyramid. On level #1, you will write the word "KNOW". This is where we will determine everything you know. I want you to now brainstorm on everything that you know how to do. What are some areas of expertise for you? At this point, we are just listing everything. We're not judging or ranking them. It doesn't matter if you love doing it or hate it. We just want to take as exhaustive an inventory of all you know as possible.

Do you know how to write? Do you know how to cook? Are you skilled with taking care of pets? Are you gifted in numerology? Are you an expert quilt maker? List everything. For the sake of this example, I'll just list three. Let's say I know how to build websites, know how to cook, and know how to market books. So, I would write those down next to #1. In Secret #2, we will begin sorting through the list, but for now your pyramid should look something like this:

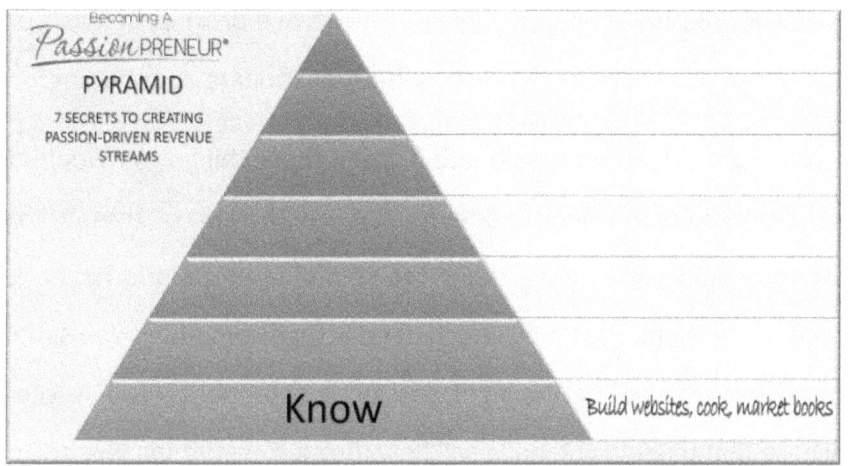

SECRET #2: PURSUE YOUR PASSION

Becoming a Passionpreneur simply means taking those things you're passionate about and growing them into a business? Let's go back to the list of things you know. Let's look at all the things you wrote down that you know and ask yourself, which of those things are you actually passionate about? Because like I told you earlier, I can build websites. I know how to build websites, but I don't like doing it. I hate building them for other people. I don't really like doing them for myself. Since we are not interested in doing anything that doesn't excite us about waking up each day, we are only going to build a business model around that which we are passionate.

Let's take a look at the list of things we know from Secret #1. Hopefully, you wrote down five or more things you know. The next step is to choose the two or three things you know that you are most passionate about. In the next space above KNOW, you want to write

"PASSION". Beside that, you want to list the two or three things from your things you know list that you're most passionate about doing.

When we talk about passionate, I mean those things you would do for free if you didn't need money to survive. The two or three things that you could see yourself doing the rest of your life and never get bored doing them. Passion is much deeper than something you simply like or enjoy. Choosing the right passion is essential to your success because that passion you have will flow through everything you do and help you prosper. The marketplace will feel and respond to your passion.

I'll choose cooking and marketing books for my example. Your Passionpreneur Pyramid should look like this now:

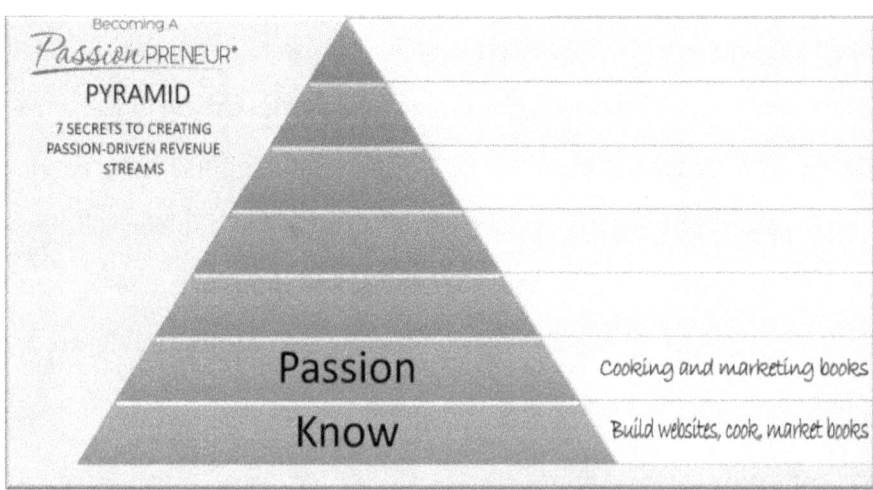

SECRET #3: CHASE PURPOSE NOT PROFITS

We've been discussing how to build passion-driven revenue streams throughout the book, but Secret #3 is probably one of the most important lessons in the entire process. While business is about generating revenue and making money, your goal as a Passionpreneur should be to chase purpose, not profits. What does that mean?

Of course, if you are in business, your goal is to make profits. Otherwise, you wouldn't need to start a business. But much like we all have a purpose for our lives, your business should also have a purpose. You see many businesses express their purpose in the form of a vision and/or mission statement. Your business purpose should be something you can easily share with anyone who asks, and it should be your guiding light as you grow.

You're in business to make profit, but you're not chasing profits. There must be a purpose for your business. There must be a purpose for your money other than just stuffing your pockets. So, ask yourself and write it down. "What is the purpose for my business?" Not your life's purpose. Don't get it confused. Your life's purpose is not always going to be exactly the same as your business purpose. But ask yourself, what is your business purpose? Why are you starting this business? Because you don't *have* to be in business. And more than likely there is someone else who already does what you do or something similar to it. It's your business purpose that will differentiate you from the competition.

Knowing your business purpose also helps keep you focused. There are a million and one ways to make money. When you're chasing profits, you will find yourself trying all million and one ways to get money. When you are chasing purpose, money will start chasing YOU in a million and one ways. You must avoid constantly trying to jump to the next big money-making scheme and next new fad. There will always be someone who appears to be succeeding faster than you, making more money than you, going more places than you, and undoubtedly you will begin to question if you're doing the right thing. If you allow yourself to get too distracted by the journey of others around you, it can cause you to lose direction on your own journey.

If you haven't done so already, go to the third row and write "Purpose". Next to that, write a one sentence description of the purpose of your business. The purpose isn't simply *what* your business does. The purpose should encompass *why* your business does it. What greater good is your business serving. I'm going to use the cooking example and state the purpose for my cooking business to be "To provide easy, healthy meal planning options for single parents in order to combat childhood obesity".

Once you develop the purpose for your business, go ahead and write it on the purpose line of the pyramid. Read it aloud. Does it resonate with you? Does it motivate you? Most importantly, is it a true statement? Once you're set on your business purpose, complete that line on your pyramid and let's move to Secret #4.:

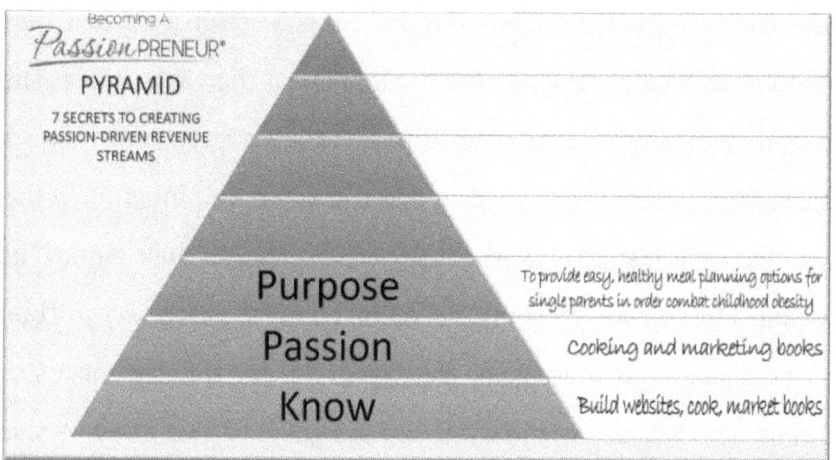

SECRET #4: GIVE GIVE GIVE!!!!

The next secret is to give, give, give. In business, we need to make sure we are constantly giving. What should we be giving? We need to give content. We need to give value. We need to give excellence. We need to give above and beyond what we promised. We are in a Giver's Economy. The companies that give the most, will be in position to receive the most. Have you ever searched for some information from an expert in something you were trying to do and they drew you in with a great headline like "I'm going to teach you everything you need to know about XYZ!"? And you click the link thinking "Oh great! I've been looking for this!" Then you get to the site and they tell you, "I'll give you what you came for, as soon as you pay me $5,000." Ever had that happen? You're like, "Why would I pay you $5,000? I don't even know what you're offering. I don't even know you. You haven't given me anything."

As entrepreneurs, you can't just tell people, "Hurry up and buy!" anymore. Consumers are much more intelligent than in the past. They have far too many tools at their disposal to investigate your claims as well as find someone else making a better offer. You must build their trust. You can't just go and expect people to give you their money, not knowing who you are. You must build that credibility. One way you build it is by giving. You must give, give, give. So, for this section of the pyramid, you will determine what you are going to give away. Yes, for free.

I can hear you now. "But Ryan, if I give it away, they will just take the freebies and not buy anything. I can't afford to give anything away." Let me stop you there. When you're building a business, you cannot build with a scarcity mindset. You cannot be afraid to give something away for fear there will be nothing left. If that were true, then you shouldn't be in business to begin with. How would the world know how delicious bourbon chicken tastes, if the restaurants were too afraid to give away samples in every mall food court across America? The truth of the matter is, there is an abundance of ideas, resources, valuable content, and even bourbon chicken, you can release for free, knowing that will open doors to greater returns.

Look at this book. I've offered several free items all throughout it. The Passionpreneur Pyramid you're currently completing (you did download it, right?) is a free item. Do you think I lost more than I stand to gain by giving you that resource for free? I doubt it. So, what are some things you could create and give away for free in order to generate leads and possible customers? A few ideas include, surveys, assessments, videos, trainings, white papers, eBooks, audio books, webinars, the list goes on and on. For my example, I'm going to give away free weekly recipes and instructional videos on YouTube. Can you imagine how powerful that would be if every week single parents were flocking to my site to watch free videos and get recipes for their weekly meals? How long do you think it would take before they were begging for more in-depth content they'd be willing to pay for? If you want to sell more, you must first give more.

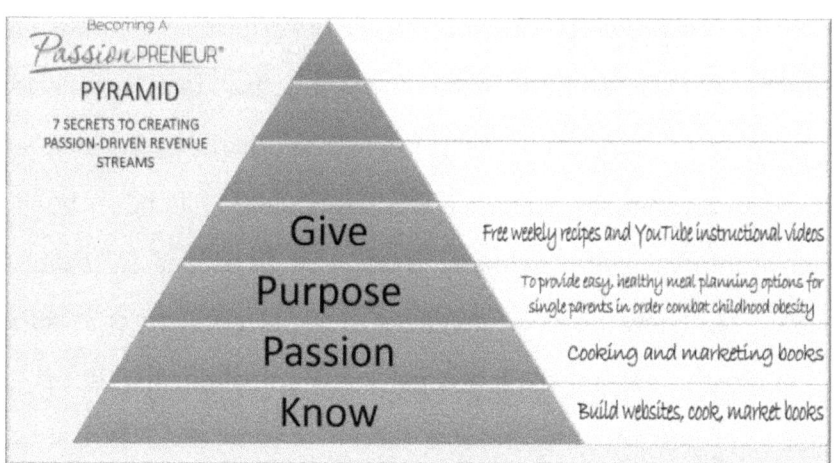

SECRET #5: THE FIERCE URGENCY OF NOW

I love Martin Luther King Jr. He was always one of my role models growing up. I still try to model myself after him as much as I can. He talked about the fierce urgency of now. How does that relate to becoming a Passionpreneur? Your fierce urgency must be directed towards figuring out what you can launch NOW. Have you ever had a great idea and sat on it while you were perfecting it then you look up and someone else does it before you? I experienced that recently. There was an idea I had about six years ago, but I wasn't in a position to make it happen. During that time, someone else came along and launched "my" idea! All I could do was watch like, "Oh my goodness, that was my idea!" But here's the thing. Your product, your idea, your offering doesn't have to be perfect for you to launch it. But you must launch it in order to perfect it.

A few years ago, I partnered with a small business consultancy owned by Che Brown and Trevor Otts, Peak Performers Institute. One of the things I learned from Team PPI was it doesn't take a whole year of planning to launch a successful event. With them, an idea was birthed and within 30 - 90 days it was happening! I had never been in an environment where so many ideas went from idea to reality so quickly. They knew the idea didn't have to be perfect in order to launch it. The most important thing was getting it out of our minds, off the paper, and out into the universe before anyone else. Once it was launched, we could evaluate what needed to change, what worked, and what didn't work so next time we could make it better. Things were never perfect for launches, but we launched it. We were in business!

Secret #5 is focused on getting you in business. We are going to pull those ideas off the shelf and with fierce urgency, plan what we will launch in the next 90 days. What is it that you've been planning but felt like it's just not ready yet? I want to challenge you to launch that in the next 90 days. If you're serious about changing your life and making a living doing what you love, then let's evaluate what you have at your disposal right now that you can launch 90 days from today. Remember, it doesn't have to be perfect to launch it, but you must launch it to perfect it.

Ninety days from today you need to be launching something. Write it down right now. What are you launching? You've already listed what you know. We've weeded those down to just your passions. You're clear on the purpose of your business and why you want to do it. You've already figured out what you're giving away to draw people in. It's time to put it all together and launch.

Maybe you want to launch an online course. Maybe you want to write and launch your book. Maybe you want to go out and start a cooking academy for young kids. Whatever it is, 90 days, that's what you have. Stop thinking you have to wait and wait and wait. No more "I don't have money. I don't have a studio. I don't have this and that." You're never going to have it if you don't launch.

Here's what could happen when you launch. Using my example, let's say I've been dreaming about doing cooking videos but wanted to wait until I could afford matching pots and pans. I finally say, "Forget it, I'm launching anyway." People start watching my videos and someone says "He's doing a cooking show, but his pots don't even match. I'm going to donate pots and pans so the next videos he makes looks better." Whereas you would have never had those pots and pans donated, had you not just launched it in spite of your hesitation.

True story- back in maybe 2008, I had an idea for a kid's fitness DVD. I wanted kids to have a fitness program they could do that was led by my kids. It took me SIX YEARS to launch that idea. At first, I didn't launch it because my kids were too young. Then, I went through a divorce and I didn't launch anything. I quit everything for like four years. When I finally got back to being myself and creating, I said, "Okay, I have to finally do this thing." I didn't have any money to fund a project the size I had in mind, but I launched it. I started telling people about it and one day, a very good friend offered to front the money to shoot the videos. Had I not launched, that blessing would have never happened.

We shot the videos over two days, created a commercial, and we released the *FitLife Kids DVD* in 2014. Admittedly, I am a low-key perfectionist. If I'm being honest, I wasn't totally pleased with the final product. But at that point I had been promoting and advertising the DVD so I had no choice but to follow through and release the videos. The response was unbelievable! The DVD was better received by customers than I ever expected. My kids and I were featured on the local news and radio and the three of us got to work together on a family business project. All because we launched!

It's your turn now. Stop making excuses. Be afraid and do it anyway! Decide now what you will launch in the next 90 days and do it! In my fictitious scenario, I have decided to launch a Video Cookbook Series. Over the next 90 days, I will be setting up my YouTube channel, choosing recipes to feature, getting graphics designed, securing a shoot location setting up my systems... wait... that's Secret #6. For now, here's what my Passionpreneur Pyramid looks like:

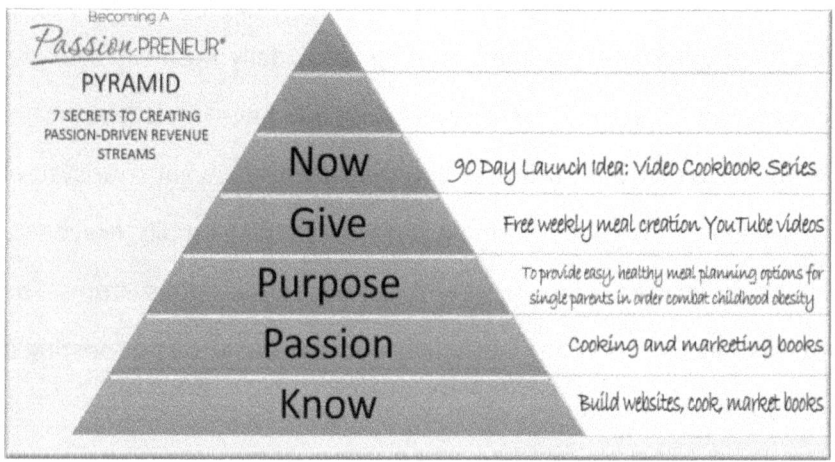

SECRET #6: PUT THE RIGHT SYSTEMS IN PLACE

I almost spilled the beans at the end of Secret #5, but Secret #6 is all about putting the right systems in place to allow you to remove yourself and your labor from your business as soon as possible. If you remember back to the lessons on when to quit your day job, I mentioned benchmarks like duplicating and automating your efforts as things that need to be in place before you quit. This is where that all comes together. Far too many entrepreneurs are solopreneurs. Everything in their business must be manually or physically done by them. It's an exhausting place to be and a terrible business model for long-term success and freedom. The goal of a Passionpreneur is to automate as much of your business so you can generate passive passion-driven revenue streams.

We talked about our launch, but the next question is how are we going to get it out to the masses? Here's where many entrepreneurs mess up. This is where I was weak for far too long in my business. You must have automated systems running your daily business activities. What are your systems? What systems do you have in place right now to help you grow your business? You may not know what your systems are. You may think your system right now is sending emails. Maybe you think it's social media. Email lists and social media are not systems. They are tools, cogs in the system. But just sending newsletters or posting on Facebook is not a system.

Oxford Dictionary defines systems as "a set of things working together as parts of a mechanism or an interconnecting network". Your business should have several parts all working together to keep your business moving and growing with minimal input and labor from you. It takes a substantial amount of work in the beginning setting up the many systems your business needs, but the payoff is, once it's done, it's done. You can, as they say in the infomercials, set it and forget it.

Another major benefit of having the right systems run your business is no prospect falls through the cracks. Every prospect who engages with your business systems gets treated the same exact way and they get the same exact presentation and communications. Your systems aren't fickle like humans. Your systems don't have bad days and treat customers nasty. Your systems don't forget to follow up. Your systems aren't afraid to ask for the sale and overcome objections. Systems are the great equalizer in business. If you are building a passion-driven business, but are afraid to sell, the systems will sell for you. If you work a demanding full-time job and don't have time to stay on top of all your client follow ups, your systems will follow up for you. This isn't where you want to allow you ego get in the way of your success. Your business doesn't need you doing everything yourself all every time. The faster you fire yourself and hire systems to do the job for you, the faster your business will grow.

Just like our body has several systems working together (i.e. digestive, respiratory, skeletal, etc.), your business has several systems you need to put in place. The amount of detail on how to do it all is far too great to share in this format. I will share the systems and what they are here, but for more help with setting up your personal systems, you can schedule your personal Passionpreneur Discovery Call by going to www.PassionpreneurDiscovery.com. In that call we can discuss best options for getting your systems setup and running.

The first system any passion-driven business needs is a Lead Generation System. This system includes your free gifts from Secret #4 to give away to prospects to encourage them to give you their information and enter your sales funnel. Your Lead Generation System also must include a squeeze page that captures prospect names and emails. That information must go to your email marketing, text communication, or CRM systems. That leads to the second system- Email Marketing System. There are tons of email marketing services on the market. You want one that allows you to generate autoresponders that will send out messages you crafted to prospects at specific times and either has its own CRM (Customer Relationship Manager) tool, or syncs to a CRM you like. Your email marketing software will also be what you use to send all email communications to prospects and customers.

The biggest and most valuable system you need is your Sales Funnel System. The Sales Funnel System is the system that walks prospect through your entire sales process. Have you ever taken advantage of an online offer where you maybe watched a video or read one of those super-long sales letters and purchased something? Then after you made your purchase, you were immediately asked if you wanted to upgrade to a more expensive offering. If you declined the offer, then a lower offer was made available? Or maybe you checked out an offer, added to your cart, changed your mind and didn't purchase. Then you get an email saying something like "Hey, you forgot to complete your purchase." All of those processes are part of a well-structured sales funnel. In a good sales funnel, you will find a squeeze page, the presentation, an upsell, a downsell, an abandoned cart feature, sales processing, and follow up. Sales funnels can be pretty expensive to setup properly, but the payoff is always worth it.

One final system I'll cover is your Presentation System. This system has many elements from other systems but it's still its own. Webinars are a great way to earn income from your expertise. The reason most content providers don't host webinars is because they can be time consuming. Hosting automated webinars take the guess work (and labor) out of the equation. Imagine recording one perfect presentation (webinar) and knowing every single prospect is going to get that same perfect introduction to your business. That's powerful! You do the presentation once, but with automated webinars, you could be doing sales presentations every 2 hours 24 hours a day. How much faster could your business grow if you had even just 10 people on 12 webinars a day? That's 840 presentations a week. How long could you last trying to make those sales presentations on your own? That's the power of having an Automated Presentation System in place.

So, your homework for this step is to complete one of the following options:

1) Research all the software available to build your business systems;
2) Visit www.PassionpreneurDiscovery.com to schedule a systems consultation with my team;
3) Let us show you how to setup your systems in the 12-Week Becoming A Passionpreneur Mastermind;
4) Register for the Becoming A Passionpreneur Weekend Intensive and have us build the systems for you.

Whichever road you decide to take, make sure you list the systems you will need in Secret #6 of your Passionpreneur Pyramid. I've listed all the systems in my sample pyramid.

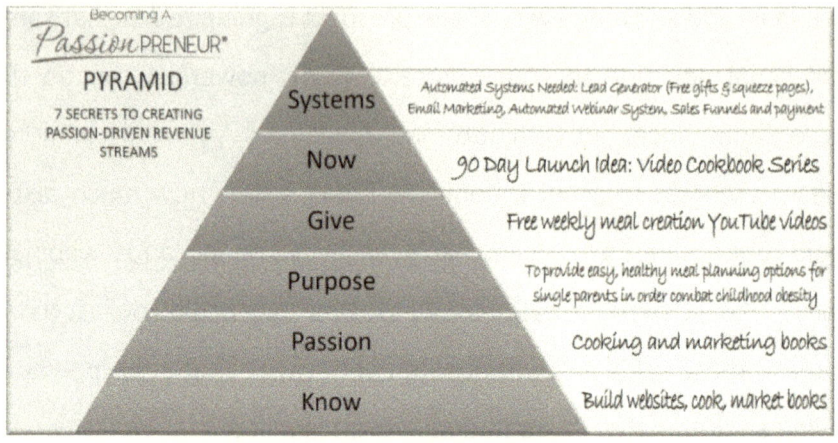

SECRET #7: LIVE YOUR STORY, TELL YOUR STORY

Live your story. Tell your story. Now we've gone through the whole pyramid. We know what we're going to launch at 90 days. We know what systems we're putting in place. Now that we've lived, it's time to create our brand and tell the story. There are many ways to tell your story. You may tell your story in book form. You may tell you a story in a video training series. You may tell your story through an album if you're a singer. You may tell your story through artwork. If you cook, you may tell your story through your cooking show. How are you going to tell your story?

When we're talking about monetizing our content, we do that through telling our story. There's a saying I learned in my network marketing days, "facts tell, stories sell". As kids, we weren't told bedtime facts, we were told bedtime stories. People love a great story. Becoming A Passionpreneur is all about telling your story as many times as you can, to as many people as you can. The systems we set up in

Secret #6 allow us to tell our story the same way every time and way more often than we could tell it ourselves.

All of my books are transparent. My books are my story. I write as if I'm teaching the lessons to the person reading the book, but I am always the first student. It's my story. I had to live and experience those things first, and then tell my story and be able to monetize it. My most recent story is this book you're reading now, *Becoming A Passionpreneur.* I lived it and now I'm telling it.

So, what's the title of *your* story? Take the time now and pick the name for your story. If you were writing a book today, what would the title be? Write your book title right now. If you're starting a TV show, write the title down. Maybe you will start a podcast. That's easy! It doesn't cost any money. You can go online and start a podcast TODAY! You could tell your story every week, every day, 15 minutes a day. What's the name of your new podcast? My podcast is called *The Passionpreneur Podcast*. It's available on iTunes, Spotify, iHeart Radio, and Google Podcasts and it doesn't cost me anything to produce. (I would love for you to subscribe to the show and leave a 5-star review and a comment.)

Here's where my true passion lies. I love assisting people with telling their story through books. For 15 years I've helped authors craft their books and market them to the masses. As a Passionpreneur, writing your book will open up countless doors to opportunities to spread your message while also generating multiple streams of income. If you are interested in learning how to write and market your book, I want to work with you. Writing and publishing books is nowhere near as burdensome a task as it was even just 15 years ago, but there are still secrets to doing it right.

My company, Indie Author PRO, offers numerous resources for independent authors that will maximize your profits. When you are ready to write your story, or if you've already written it but need help selling it, be sure to visit www.IndieAuthorPRO.com and see how we can help with that.

So, getting back to our example, let's bring it all together. I listed everything I know that I could teach others. I decided I was most passionate about cooking. Determined my business purpose would be to help single parents meal prep as a way to combat childhood obesity. I plan to give away recipes via weekly You Tube instructional videos. I'm going to launch my video cookbook series in 90 days. I have designed and built all the systems I need to market, sell, generate leads, and communicate once my launch happens. I've decided to tell my story in the form of a video cookbook series. All I need now is a title. Let's call it "Single & Cooking for Kids". That's now my brand. Everywhere I go, I begin telling my story through my new brand, "Single & Cooking for Kids". You want to tell your story so much that your name becomes synonymous with your brand/story. On the top level of the Passionpreneur Pyramid, write your brand name. Write the title to your story and three means by which you plan to tell it.

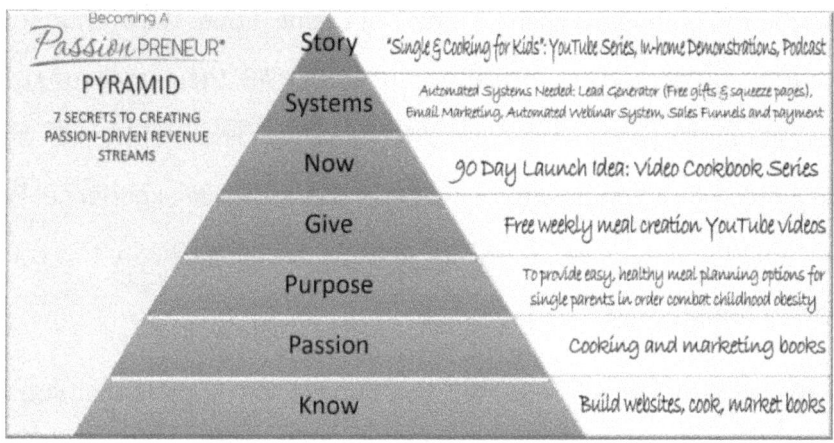

You did it! You learned the Seven Secrets to Creating Passion-Driven Revenue Streams! I know that was a lot of information condensed into a few pages, but that is the system in a nutshell. You can use this system to launch your idea into a viable automated revenue stream. At this point you have a big decision to make. You must decide if you want to 1) take this journey alone; 2) partner with my team and have us walk you through it in one of our upcoming 12-Week Passionpreneur Masterminds; or 3) have my team do it all for you over a weekend and you walk out with a whole new Passionpreneur business in a "box" up and running for you.

If you choose Option #1 and do it yourself, awesome! I can't wait to hear your success stories! Join our Passionpreneur Facebook Group at www.facebook.com/groups/thepassionpreneurs and get support from our community of likeminded Passionpreneurs. If you choose Option #2 and would like information on joining the next mastermind, simply visit my website www.ryancgreene.com and click "COURSES" for information on how you can be a part of the next one. We only do four a year. If you're ready to rock and want Option #3, then email me right away at ryan@ryancgreene.com with the subject line "INTENSIVE" and you'll receive info on how to be a part of this exclusive experience. We only hold two intensives a year for only six people each. So, this is for serious inquiries only.

Regardless of which next step you choose, my hope is that you at least get started. You have the tools in your hand to succeed. The only difference between you and anyone else reading this book, is one of you will do the work and become a Passionpreneur, while the other sits the book down without applying any of it. Which reminds me... did you download the Passionpreneur Pyramid from bit.ly/BAPPyramid yet?!

THE PASSIONPRENEUR PRODUCT MATRIX

What we're going to do in this chapter is learn about and create your Passionpreneur Product Matrix. I'm going to show you how to take your one idea and turn it into a product matrix, or full suite of products, that will help generate the passion-driven revenue we've been discussing throughout the book. This section is going to require you to put in some work again, so please go ahead and make sure that you've downloaded your Passionpreneur Product Matrix worksheet at http://bit.ly/BAPMatrix. I've included a blank copy here, but you really are going to want to download the full-sized version to use. You're going to complete this matrix in this chapter so you will need the worksheet so you can take notes for yourself. The plan is to give you a foundation by showing you what types of products should be, what the price points should be, and what they should provide. If you want help with developing your products and actually building out your product suite, then schedule your Passionpreneur Discovery Session today at www.PassionpreneurDiscovery.com.

Passion PRENEUR® PRODUCT MATRIX

PRODUCT TYPE	PRICING	PURPOSE	PRODUCT OFFERING

ryan c. greene .com

So, let's jump into the product matrix. If you didn't download your matrix template, just go ahead and draw yours. You can draw it on a regular sheet of paper. The first thing you will notice on the product matrix is there are four columns. We're going to talk about the type of products you want to offer. We're going to talk about how to price those offerings. We're going to talk about the purpose behind each type of offering. Then I'm going to give you some ideas on the actual type of products that would go at each level.

So far, we have found out what you know and what you're passionate, as well as discussed steps you will take to launch your 90-day campaign. Our focus to this point has been on the one means by which you are going to transform your expertise into revenue. The purpose of the Product Matrix is to now map out the many ways we are going to create content based on your expertise and monetize said content. There are six levels of products you will create for your full suite of products and/or services. Having your project matrix set before you start business keeps you clear on exactly what your offerings are and will lead your marketing and sales funnel efforts. Once you have the matrix in place, you know exactly how each prospect should flow through your business.

RELEASES

The first product types we're going to create is your RELEASES. Your releases are the things that you're going to put out to stay fresh and draw in prospects. If you were a singer, your release would be your new album. Your releases are your products that you're putting out there that are going to help give the market something new to consume. Something that you can offer people who took advantage of your freebies to purchase right now. You only need one release at a time per brand. Singers don't release 4 separate singles at once and you don't want to release four new books at once.

Here's how you price your release. Your release can range in price anywhere from $17 to $97. You want your "buy now" offers to be under $100 so there isn't much of a buying decision that needs to be made. You may sell an eBook for $37. Maybe you're offering an introductory master class for $97. You could offer an audio program for $17. Your release is going to be the introductory offer you promote on a regular basis. It's the gateway into your sales funnel. Again, it doesn't have to be that you're always releasing something new. You may have only one release, but that release is your introduction you're constantly promoting to draw in prospects.

The purpose of your releases is to provide immediate value to the buyer. You want to give the prospect something of value from jump. What your release also does is immediately position you as an expert. It makes you an authority on the subject matter you're teaching. People will look at you totally different if you're claiming to be an expert but all you do is tweet about it, versus if you have actual published product on your subject matter.

So, what are some examples of releases you could have? I'll use myself as an example. One of my releases is my "101 Secrets To Sell More Books Now" audio training program. It's a recorded training where I teach 101 secrets to help authors sell more books and triple their book sales. The product is always available through my Indie

Author PRO program. It's a digital product, so I don't have to press CDs. The sales process is automated, so I don't have to go out there and physically sell it every time. People can automatically download it and once they do, they enter my product matrix sales sequence. It's a $37 audio product release.

Other products you may use as releases could be eBooks, audios, videos, or traditional books. The main thing to remember is you're setting yourself up as someone who possesses valuable knowledge and expertise about something your prospect wants or needs. In that vein, you must be sure you are providing quality valuable content. The idea isn't to simply create something to sell. You want to create something that brings value to the marketplace. Quantity isn't the goal here. Quality is what we're after. Don't be like those rappers who puts 24 songs on their double CD and only 7 songs are bangers. Make every one of your releases that hot fire!

Here's a secret if you haven't already figured it out. This book you're reading right now is also a release. While I sell the book by various means, the main distribution channel is through the sales page set up at www.Passionpreneurbook.com. If you didn't purchase the book from that site, I encourage you to visit so you can see what my book release page looks like. If you're interested in getting help setting up a page of your own for your book, visit www.Passionpreneurdiscovery.com to schedule a discovery session so we can discuss best ways to get you rolling.

Passion PRENEUR®
PRODUCT MATRIX

PRODUCT TYPE	PRICING	PURPOSE	PRODUCT OFFERING
Releases	$17 - $97	Deliver value. Position self as expert.	CD, eBook, Audio, Video, Book

RENEWALS

The next product we're going to create is some sort of RENEWAL. You want to create some product to offer that customers are paying for monthly. A renewal product price can range anywhere from $9 a month up to $97 a month. Every month you're going to provide some form of content or information via a subscription service in which your customers are enrolled.

Renewals help in a couple of ways. First, renewals help you to generate predictable recurring revenue. With renewals, you know every month what your income baseline is. If you have one hundred people subscribed to virtual book club for $9/month, then you know the first of every month, you have $900 in the bank. One of the biggest challenges any entrepreneur faces is trying to figure out where their next check is coming from. Entrepreneurs must go out every day and create income. When you have some type of renewal product, when people are subscribing to you monthly, it helps you know each month there's at least some level of guaranteed income there.

Secondly, renewals also help you stay in front of your audience. It gives them new content every month, so they never forget about you and they stay tuned in to what you're providing. Renewals also help you build your tribe. When you have a growing group who you are pouring into every single month, they become your ambassadors and the best sales team you could ever find. It gets people following you and becoming true disciples, as opposed to them simply grabbing your release and never using it.

Product offerings for renewals could include a membership portal. You host a private-members only section of your site where only paid members have access to exclusive content. As an author, you may set up a virtual book club. Instead of selling your book for $20 and that's it, readers could join your virtual book club for $9/month and go through the book with you monthly. Your $20 book now becomes a $108 book. Maybe you have a mastermind where people can join and for the next 12 months get content sent to them along with two phone sessions a month. You can have live teleconferences that allow for Q & A sessions. There are so many options.

What we're doing as we progress through the product matrix is building our credibility as we go. People aren't going to buy your $37 release and then jump to spend $10,000 on an offering. It doesn't happen that way. With this process, we're taking baby steps and bringing people through our matrix as they commit to a little bit of us at a time. The goal is to get them in the habit of giving something to get something while we're developing ourselves as an expert. We want to build confidence along the way so they begin to believe, 1) that we know we're talking about; 2) that we can deliver on our promises; and 3) that we can truly help them to achieve their goals. Patiently, but deliberately, walking each customer through your product matrix cycle will allow for the best success in getting a "Yes" from them.

PassionPRENEUR® PRODUCT MATRIX

PRODUCT TYPE	PRICING	PURPOSE	PRODUCT OFFERING
Releases	$17 - $97	Deliver value. Position self as expert.	CD, eBook, Audio, Video, Book
Renewals	$9/mo - $97/mo	Build predictable recurring revenue	Membership portals, subscription services

ryan c. greene .com

RAPPORT BUILDERS

I call the next product type you RAPPORT BUILDERS. Now that you know people will spend $17 - $97 and give you a shot, you can begin offering them the next level service or product. What your rapport builders do is simply help customers trust you without them having to bet the farm on you. Rapport builder products provide an introductory step for people to be a part of your system. These are slightly higher priced items and now require people to make some level of commitment. They said, "Yes" to your release for under $100. They said, "Yes" to your renewals for under $100/mo. Now they want to take a baby step towards the next level with you.

Walking prospects through your sales process is like dating. First you hold their hand, then you get a kiss on the cheek, then you may get a peck on the lips. Your entire process should be built to get a series of "yeses" from prospects. Stop trying to meet someone the first day and get married. At least meet for coffee and a conversation first. Your rapport building products give prospects a means by which to "try you out" while also getting something of value in return.

The price range for this level should be anywhere from $127 - $497. At this price point, customers are making their first level of real commitment. People aren't just going to throw $500 at any expert with a video online. Your rapport builders must provide some type of valuable service and offering that's worth this kind of ask. These are your entry level services, but these are vital to future success.

Don't underestimate the importance of this product line level. This is the fulcrum upon which your entire business balances. This is the make or break stage of most content-based businesses. If you provide amazing content and value here, people will clamor for more. If you provide boo-boo because you're putting profit over purpose, you'll lose them every time, and this will be where all your clients stop. One of the best benefits of using this system is it gives you instant feedback on the quality of your offerings. If clients aren't moving past a certain stage, you know right away where you need to focus your efforts and change some things.

At this point, your clients have made several small purchases. So far, you've been giving your customers information and telling them to go do it on their own. Rapport building services introduce the idea of getting customers started working *with* you. It's how you begin transitioning customers to becoming clients. At this level, products you can offer include mini-masterminds, conferences, consultations, or any other type of introductory service. An introductory service is something where you're not giving them everything, but you're giving them something to get them started.

If your business is brand building, an introductory service may be a photoshoot or logo design package. Or, you can offer a call and give a 60-minute consultation for a couple of hundred dollars. These are introductory services. Clients won't walk away with everything, but they do walk away with something tangible they learned or gained from you, and they also have gotten their first taste of working with you as their expert.

One of my entry level Rapport Building products is the Passionpreneur Start Lab (www.PassionpreneurAcademy.com). The Starter Lab is a digital membership portal where you can get special training to kickstart your journey to becoming a Passionpreneur. It's a beginner level training program but it packs a wallop that delivers great value to those who enroll. That's the rapport we're building. Once your clients fall in love with you, then you can invite them out to the fancy restaurants and the next level of your product matrix.

Passion PRENEUR® PRODUCT MATRIX

PRODUCT TYPE	PRICING	PURPOSE	PRODUCT OFFERING
Releases	$17 - $97	Deliver value. Position self as expert.	CD, eBook, Audio, Video, Book
Renewals	$9/mo - $97/mo	Build predictable recurring revenue	Membership portals, subscription services
Rapport Builders	$197 - $497	Entry level service to gain trust	Conference, consults, low-level programs

ryan c. greene .com

REACHABLE SOLUTIONS

Your next product line is what I call REACHABLE SOLUTIONS. What do I mean by that? Reachable Solutions are, as the name signifies, solutions that can be reached. Here is the trap you don't want to fall into. You don't want to fall into the trap of making offers and claims that you can't back up and/or you can't help enough people regularly achieve.

If I was claiming that I was going to help struggling authors all become millionaire authors, while that sounds good and most people would love to be millionaires, the truth of the matter is most authors won't ever become millionaires. They can't even fathom becoming a millionaire. It's not something most can do right now. But, a promise to help authors complete a book in 30 days? That's reachable. That's something people who enroll in my 30-Day Indie Author Challenge walk away with. In 30 days, they will write and be ready to release their books.

When we talk about reachable solutions, we want to determine what are some milestones we have the expertise and the capacity to help people reach right now? We want to promote a product or service that can impact someone's life or business immediately. These offerings will focus on specific areas of someone's life or business. You're not going to change the whole thing. You're not going to do an entire makeover. You're not going to do an entire business launch for your client. You're going to change one thing and make that great, so they don't have to worry about it. Maybe you offer to show how to setup their webinar and sales funnel. Going back to our earlier example of cooking for single parents, you may offer a 3-month meal-prep service. This service should be your bread-and-butter service.

Your reachable solutions should range from $597 to $1,997. Just under $2,000 should be the max for your reachable solutions. For most individuals and small business owners, $2,000 is going to be a significant investment. While a significant investment, expectations should remain realistic. You shouldn't be promising clients they will make a million dollars by investing in your $2,000 product. Teaching how they could earn an extra $3,000 or more a month using your expertise would be a more realistic expectation. If you're in the health and wellness space, you may charge $697 for a 60-day weight loss challenge where you include meal plans, supplements and workouts, with the goal clients will lose 20 pounds. Whatever your promise is at this level, you need to be able to deliver on it and your client should walk away with something tangible they can look at and say was completed for them.

Your rapport builders should be your bread and butter offering. It's the thing you want to become known for doing. This is where you really make your money. When people say they need someone who can do XYZ, you want them to automatically think of your company as the ones to do it. When satisfied clients refer you to their network, it will be your reachable solutions they recommend first. A great product to develop for this level is building your own digital academy or online learning portal. A digital academy full of your training and knowledge allows clients to access your wisdom without you having to physically teach them in person. I have a Becoming A Passionpreneur Academy as well as an Indie Author PRO Academy. Each digital academy offers different levels of membership at different price levels, with access to different content.

If you're teaching about leadership, what can you put in place right here? What kind of a system can you offer for $597 to $,1997 that's going to really produce results? At this level you must do more than teach concepts. You must have some track record and proof of results that you can show. People aren't going to pay thousands of dollars just to hear you teach on theory. You must be able to show them how they can implement your content in their business or life.

At this level, you must be prepared to share the nuts and bolts of your systems and be ready to walk your clients through a deeper level of training. You may have plenty of content and expertise on something, but if you cannot show people how to turn that into something that can actually earn results for their business, or their lives, then you're going to drop the ball at this level every time. This product level is where you really want to spend time developing strong offerings. This Reachable Solutions will make or break your business.

Passion PRENEUR®
PRODUCT MATRIX

PRODUCT TYPE	PRICING	PURPOSE	PRODUCT OFFERING
Releases	$17 - $97	Deliver value. Position self as expert.	CD, eBook, Audio, Video, Book
Renewals	$9/mo - $97/mo	Build predictable recurring revenue	Membership portals, subscription services
Rapport Builders	$197 - $497	Entry level service to gain trust	Conference, consults, low-level programs
Reachable Solutions	$597 - $1,997	Mid-level services Bread & butter solutions	"Done with you" solutions, digital academy

ryan c. greene .com

REVENUE MAXIMIZERS

The next two levels are going to be more exclusive. As you can see, the more expensive the investment, the closer clients get to you. We're not giving one-on-one brand building sessions to $97 clients. It's not that we don't value those clients, but it's simply not the best use of our time. That's why your first few levels of the product matrix should be as automated as possible. Once we start getting to higher levels of investment, we begin working more with, and eventually for, our clients. I call this next level our REVENUE MAXIMIZERS. At this level, you're not going to have as many clients, but when you get the clients here it's going to be worth it because of the price point.

Our revenue maximizers price point goes from $2,497 to $9,997. At this point, if you're charging someone $2,500 to $10,000, you're going to have some in-person servicing. They're going to have higher access to you. Theses high-end services are not digital. You have to actually work with and for these clients. That's why you won't have as many clients here. You won't have that kind of time.

Depending on what you do, bringing in a hundred clients a year to work with individually at this level, is going to be tough to do and still provide greats experiences for them all. When you get these clients, this is where you really want to make sure you're providing the excellent service that you know someone who's paying you almost $10,000 expects to receive. The last thing you want is to overcommit yourself and have clients asking for $10,000 refunds because you got greedy and didn't perform.

The revenue maximizers is where you want to create your WOW! moments. These are the services that clients should leave you saying, "WOW! I never knew I could have this! WOW! I never knew I could do this for my business. WOW! I really feel like now I can go out here and achieve more than ever before." That's what clients should walk away feeling once they've purchased your revenue maximizers.

Another purpose these services serve is they give you your unfair advantage in the marketplace. You don't want to be a copycat here. When you're providing your revenue maximizers, you want to be THE cat. You want to be the only one doing it like you're doing it. If you find that you're not the only one, you better be the best one. You better be the one setting the bar.

This is where you're going to have your weekend intensives, you're one-on-one coaching, your exclusive small group retreats. These offering should all be small groups with no more than 8-10 people. These are the events where you are getting in and working intimately with clients. My Becoming A Passionpreneur Weekend Intensive (the flyer is in the back of the book) is an example of a revenue maximizer type event. The event costs $4,997, is three-days, only accepts 6 people per class, and is only held 2-3 times a year. During the weekend, clients will work on building their Passionpreneur businesses and walk away with the entire brand built, their systems in place, sales copy written, their... well I said the flyer is in the back of the book. You can read it to see everything they get. Believe me, it will make you say "WOW!"

Maybe you can't think of how you would develop a $10,000 product. Maybe you've never thought someone would pay you that much money to learn what you know. It's okay if you don't have your $10K product yet. Your plan should be to go find someone's coaching to help you develop your program. You need to enroll in someone's program to help develop your products and develop your offerings in order to be able to become that expert worthy of charging someone $10,000.

Passion PRENEUR® PRODUCT MATRIX

PRODUCT TYPE	PRICING	PURPOSE	PRODUCT OFFERING
Releases	$17 - $97	Deliver value. Position self as expert.	CD, eBook, Audio, Video, Book
Renewals	$9/mo - $97/mo	Build predictable recurring revenue	Membership portals, subscription services
Rapport Builders	$197 - $497	Entry level service to gain trust	Conference, consults, low-level programs
Reachable Solutions	$597 - $1,997	Mid-level services Bread & butter solutions	"Done with you" solutions, digital academy
Revenue Maximizers	$2,497 - $9,997	High-level services WOW! Unfair Advantage	Intensives, Masterminds, Retreats, 1-on-1

ryan c. greene .com

RED-CARPET EXCLUSIVES

This is the top of the line. This is the crème de la crème. This is the Rolls Royce package. This is the RED-CARPET EXCLUSIVE product line. The Red-Carpet level is your $10K and up product/service line. I know for some people, maybe even you, charging over $10,000 is something you never even thought about. It's something that you never even considered an option for what you do. But here's thing, there are people out there who are charging it and more importantly, there are people out there who are paying it. So, if there are people out there willing to pay over $10,000 for help in something valuable to them, why wouldn't you be willing to provide a product or service that attracts some of those high-paying clients to your business?

The real fear people have isn't that people won't pay $10,000. The real fear is that most people feel like they aren't worthy of asking for $10,000, $15,000 $20,000. But when you know that you are an expert at what you do, and it's not in any arrogant kind of way, but when you know you've studied your craft, when you know you're offering value, when you know you can effectively help the people you say you're trying to help, then you know your worth and don't hesitate to demand it. You have confidence that you can go and charge $20,000 for something and not feel ashamed or like you're cheating someone.

Your red-carpet offering is going to almost always be one-on-one. Never even more than 3 people at a time. Remember, our entire Passionpreneur Product Matrix is built to automate our lower and mid-level offerings in order to remove ourselves from the labor of our business. The freer we are, the more we are able to create and take advantage of opportunities to draw in more business. But when you have someone paying you $20,000, oh they expect to see you. Not only do they expect to see you, they expect you to DO most of the work.

That's what goes on in the VIP Room. Red-carpet clients get a fully customized "Done for you" solution. Up to this point you've been teaching and providing content to the marketplace. The low-level offerings required customers to take it upon themselves to take you knowledge and do the work on their own. Your mid-level products were a hybrid of them on the own mixed with you doing it with them. Once you reach the high-end level, this is where you are doing it for them.

At this level you're doing things like product development, brand building and event launches, ghostwriting books, and things like that. Here is where you transition from being an expert to becoming a coach. Now you become the architect of someone else's brand, someone else's business. You may only get 4 or 5 of these kind of clients per year so this won't be your main source of revenue, but at $20K a pop, you see how impactful the revenue could be.

PassionPRENEUR® PRODUCT MATRIX

PRODUCT TYPE	PRICING	PURPOSE	PRODUCT OFFERING
Releases	$17 - $97	Deliver value. Position self as expert.	CD, eBook, Audio, Video, Book
Renewals	$9/mo - $97/mo	Build predictable recurring revenue	Membership portals, subscription services
Rapport Builders	$197 - $497	Entry level service to gain trust	Conference, consults, low-level programs
Reachable Solutions	$597 - $1,997	Mid-level services Bread & butter solutions	"Done with you" solutions, digital academy
Revenue Maximizers	$2,497 - $9,997	High-level services WOW! Unfair Advantage	Intensives, Masterminds, Retreats, 1-on-1
Red Carpet Exclusives	$10,000 +	One-on-One Exclusive Attention	Customized "Done for you" solutions

ryan c. greene .com

That is the Passionpreneur Product Matrix. This is where it all starts. This is where the magic happens. This is how you take your one little $17 release and turn your content into a six-figure passion-driven revenue stream. Do you see how powerful this tool can be for exploding your business? I cannot make any income promises, but even if you only had TWO clients purchase the high-end of each level, that's over $60K your passion just generated in revenue for you in a year. This is why getting paid for what you know, is so much more profitable than getting paid for what you do.

You now have the tools to build your own product matrix. As you develop your products, remember to focus on purpose, not profits. As long as you chase purpose, profits will chase you. You don't want to ask, "What can I sell for $597?" Your question should be "What can I provide to help build rapport and how do I package that?" Then it's "How much do I charge for that?" You have everything you need to begin your journey as a Passionpreneur, young padawan. The force is strong in you.

Thank you so much for trusting me with your process and journey. I can't wait to hear your success stories!

RYAN C. GREENE

CONCLUSION

You made it! Or did you just skip to the end? I'm going to go with you made it. Congratulations! Hopefully, you didn't simply read the pages of this book, but you went through the activities, printed out the worksheets, and truly began building your passion-driven revenue streams. Becoming a Passionpreneur is no easy task, but the journey is so worth it. This isn't a process you can do in a week. You should be coming back to this book time and time again.

As you embark upon your 90-day launch you will get some things right, and undoubtedly you will discover some things that need to be tweaked. No matter what, if you get started, you're already winning. Just launching your new idea will put you ahead of 70% of Americans who hate their jobs. When you are pursuing your passions, it makes getting up every morning, just a wee bit easier.

Remember, you don't have to take this journey alone. I want to help you as much as you will allow me to help. Join the exclusive Passionpreneur Network Facebook Group at bit.ly/BAPNetwork and become a member of our tribe of Passionpreneurs. There you can get all kinds of support and resources for your journey. Follow me on all social media at @rygspeaks and let me hear your success story! If you are hosting a conference or event and would like to book me to speak, visit www.ryancgreene.com and let's make that happen.

Also, make sure you subscribe to The Passionpreneur Podcast on iTunes, Spotify, iHeart Radio, Google Podcasts or TuneIn and listen every week as we breakdown important topics and spotlight Passionpreneurs just like YOU. Make sure you take advantage of all the tools being made available to you. If you trusted me enough with your journey, the least I can do is avail myself to you as much as possible.

Finally, if this book was valuable to you and helped you re-ignite your fire you thought was lost forever, share it with a friend. Well, don't share THIS copy, tell your friends and family how to purchase their own copy at www.PassionpreneurBook.com. Become an ambassador for the Becoming A Passionpreneur system and shout us out on all your social media. Share the purchase link among your network. Also, make sure you leave a review on Amazon.com so the world knows how much you benefitted from what you learned.

I will leave you with this. When you first picked up this book, odds are, you were one of those 70% of Americans who were disengaged with work but felt you had no choice but to give up on your dreams and accept the life you had. You probably felt the best part of going to work, was getting off work. It's my hope that some part of this book awakened the dreamer in you and made you realize it is not too late to re-ignite your fire, turn your knowledge into revenue, and live your most rewarding life.

You have a gift and a passion. Life wasn't given to us to be miserable every morning when we go to work. You can make a living doing what you love. You have everything you need to become a Passionpreneur. It's time for you to go to work on your dreams and make the world know you were here!

To your success!

RYAN C. GREENE

BONUS RESOURCES

MY GOAL: _____

SACRIFICE — *What am I willing to give up in order to achieve my goal?*
_____
_____

TEAM — *Who is going to help me achieve my goal?*
_____
_____

UPLIFTING — *Where is my goal taking me that's better than where I am presently?*
_____
_____

PLAN — *How do I specifically plan to achieve my goal?*
_____
_____

INSPIRED — *Why am I going after this goal?*
_____
_____

DEADLINE — *When do I plan to achieve my goal?*
_____
_____

Text the word "STUPID" to (614) 333-0338 to download the FREE audio training "Setting S.T.U.P.I.D. Goals"

Download your free full color Passionpreneur Pyramid from
http://bit.ly/BAPPyramid

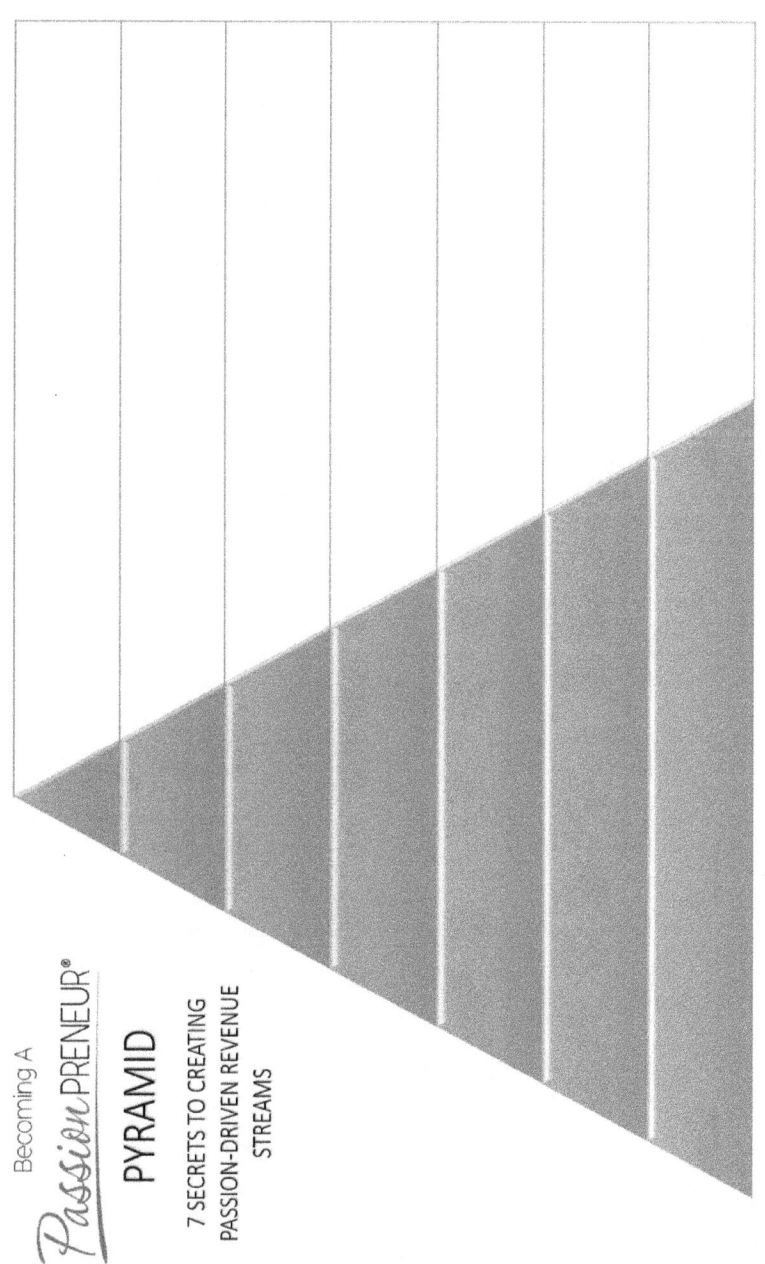

Download your free full color Passionpreneur Pyramid from
http://bit.ly/BAPMatrix

Passionpreneur® Product Matrix

PRODUCT TYPE	PRICING	PURPOSE	PRODUCT OFFERING

MEET THE PASSIONPRENEUR

Whether via a stage in front of thousands, over the radio and television airwaves, or through one of his many bestselling books, "The Passionpreneur" Ryan C. Greene develops leaders and serves as a strategic coach to authors, content experts, and entrepreneurs. Ryan empowers audiences with the knowledge and practical training to get paid for what they know by building content-based, passion-driven revenue streams. Ryan's mission is to help people break free from the chains of mediocre living and live their most successful and productive lives! Ryan helps independent authors maximize their profits from their book content with his top-rated Indie Author PRO program. Having shared stages with speaking greats like Willie Jolley, Delatorro McNeal II, Cheryl Wood, and George Fraser, Ryan is solidifying himself as one of the nation's most sought after trainers on leadership, personal development and content-based entrepreneurship. Ryan currently hosts and produces "The Passionpreneur Podcast" and the "Make It Matter" online web-series.

Ryan C. Greene is an entrepreneur, Certified Author Coach, bestselling author, and professional speaker. He is the Founder of GreeneHouse Media LLC, a media company whose goal is to provide "Media With A Purpose" via radio, television, film, and books. Ryan is the author of six books and specializes in teaching authors and speakers how to monetize their content, automate their business and boost their revenue.

In January 2005, Ryan founded Bakari Book Publishers (now GreeneHouse Media) and published his first book, <u>SUCCESS IS IN YOUR HAND: 19 Keys To Unlocking The Successful Person You Were Designed To Be</u>. His second book, <u>MY LITTLE BLACK BOOK OF LEADERSHIP: 15 Leadership Lessons I Learned From My Ex-Girlfriends</u>, was released in the March 2008. In December 2008 Ryan released his third book, _LEAD WOLF VS LONE WOLF: You're Only A Leader If Others Are Following_ followed by his fourth book, the Amazon.com #1 Best Seller, _THE QUEENS' LEGACY_ in April 2009. Ryan's fifth book _CREATE A BETTER YOU!: 12 Essential Elements For Your Greatest Comeback EVER_ was released in January 2013. His newest books _LEADERSHIP UNIVERSITY_ and _BECOMING A PASSIONPRENEUR_ were released in January 2016 in May 2019 respectively.

In January 2006, Ryan became the Executive Producer and Host of his own weekly radio talk show, **"The Ryan C. Greene Show"**. In November 2010, Ryan began co-hosting a weekly radio show, **"The Ryan and Bryan Show"**, with Bryan Johnson. Through his media company, Ryan hopes to change lives by delivering high-impact relevant solutions for unlocking one's full potential and realizing one's individual destiny and purpose. Ryan is also jumping into film and television production. He executive produced a fitness DVD for children, **"FitLife Kids"**, and is developing two game shows.

Ryan speaks from the heart and his genuine, thought provoking, and humorous presentations have already changed countless lives. He has been featured in a wide array of print, radio and television media. He has been a contributing writer for several magazines as well as guest hosted several radio and television talk shows.

Ryan graduated from Hampton University in Hampton, VA with a Bachelor of Science Degree in Marketing and earned his MBA from University of Maryland Global Campus. He has two children, Jordan and Jayden, and currently resides in Mitchellville, MD with his wife Tyneka.

For more information or to book Ryan C. Greene to speak for your organization or to present at your next event, please visit www.RyanCGreene.com

SPEAKER - AUTHOR - PASSIONPRENEUR

Book Ryan C. Greene to speak.

"...an possesses the uncanny ability to synthesize complex topics and issues of our ..., into relatable constructs and experiences. His approach truly resonates with ...iences on all levels and is proven to be highly transferable across platforms."
—...rred Hugle, VP, Supply Chain, Domino's Pizza, Inc.

"...an truly personifies what it means to be a leader. I owe much of my success ...y to the lessons I learned from him."
—...ike Powell, VP, Organizational Development & Training, Powell Consulting Group

"...an definitely makes the process of learning leadership an engaging journey."
—...latorro L. McNeal, II, MSP, Peak Performance Expert

"...an's leadership training at our Annual Leadership Development Institute ... the highest rated workshop by the attendees for five years in a row!"
—...dney Frank, Alpha Phi Alpha Fraternity, Inc.

"...an is an irrefutable force in the self-development industry. Any offering ...h him will catapult you to your unique greatness."
—...tthew C. Horne, Executive Publisher, Lightning Fast Book Publishing

ryan c. greene .com

...DERSHIP | ENTREPRENEURSHIP | MARKETING

...n C. Greene is one of the nation's ...t sought after leadership trainers. ...ing shared stages with speaking ...ts like Delatorro McNeal II, Dr. Willie ...y, and George Fraser, Ryan's talks ...ersonal and professional develop-...t, leadership, entrepreneurship, and ...d marketing, have bolstered client's ...s, re-ignited the fire within teams, ... created passion-driven leaders ...ss the globe! **Book Ryan to speak ...our audience today.**

PARTIAL TRAINING TRACKS

LEADERSHIP & PERSONAL DEVELOPMENT
Give your employees or students the tools they need to become great leaders and a stronger team.

Topics include: leadership training, staff development, team building, communication

CONTENT DEVELOPMENT & DISTRIBUTION
Hire Ryan for your next business conference to teach your audience how to turn their expertise into marketable content

Tracks include: content and product creation, content distribution & monetization, building digital academies, using webinars to grow business, hosting virtual summits

AUTHOR MARKETING & COACHING
Go from unknown hustler to profitable business owner by turning your book into a $100K revenue machine.

Tracks include: content and product development, sales copy writing mastery, lead generation and monetizing your book, media mastery, marketing automation

 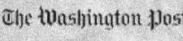    

Book Now At www.RyanCGreene.com

Subscribe to The Passionpreneur Podcast
on iTunes, Spotify, Google Podcasts, or iHeartRadio.

Interested in being a guest?
Visit www.ryancgreene.com and click the "Appointment" link to schedule an appearance

Follow Ryan C. Greene on all social media @rygspeaks

Text GOALS to (614) 333-0338 and receive a FREE audio training download

All books available at www.RyanCGreene.com

LEADERSHIP UNIVERSITY
52 Weekly Leadership Lessons On Becoming The Leader Others Will Beg To Follow

Q. What would it be like to have all of Ryan C. Greene's Leadership Lessons compiled into one book?

A. You're holding it in your hands!

Ryan C. Greene has authored 5 books and finally he has compiled all of his leadership lessons into one easy to follow leadership manual. This book of 52 leadership courses is designed to systematically assist you over the next year with your own personal leadership mastery through weekly leadership readings, knowledge application activities, and personal reflections.

Becoming a better leader has nothing to do with getting a promotion on your job. It has nothing to do with getting a new title. It has nothing to do with your boss, family, co-workers or subordinates. The first person you must learn to lead is yourself and this book is the perfect tool to assist you in that daunting task.

[PURCHASE BOOK]   [KINDLE VERSION]

CREATE A BETTER YOU!
12 Essential Elements For Your Greatest Comeback Ever

"What do you do when you are fed up with the cards you've been dealt in life? You either fold and surrender or you accept that maybe it's not the cards you've been dealt that's the problem, but rather how you have played those cards. You either go on blaming every other person, place or thing for your dissatisfaction or you look in the mirror and accept the fact that you are staring at your biggest problem."

The moment you accept that the key to you living a better life hinges on you taking responsibility for creating a better YOU is the moment you will begin to experience the fullness God has purposed for your life. Create A Better YOU! gives you 12 Essential Elements in your life to begin improving upon in order to develop yourself into a person worthy of and ready for your best life. From creating a better CONNECTION to creating a better STORY, Ryan Greene opens up and shares, through his customary transparent story telling, his keys to how you can create a better you and thereby create a better YOU in this easy to read book.

[PURCHASE BOOK]   [KINDLE VERSION]

MY LITTLE BLACK BOOK OF LEADERSHIP
15 Leadership Lessons I Learned From My EX-Girlfriends

In this half memoir, half self-help book, Ryan opens up and takes you on an intimate, funny and 100% true journey through 15 of his past relationships and shows how the lessons he learned from each ex-girlfriend can be used to shape individuals into greater leaders. Ryan's theme "You do not need a title to be a leader; you need a purpose" rings true throughout the book as he stresses the importance of becoming the leader you want to be, before your business card says you are.

This book is so vividly written that you will actually feel as if you are right there with Ryan living his life all over. If there has ever been a personal development book that reads like a movie this is that book. If you are a child of the 80's and 90's then you will love the way each chapter takes you back to that year with the timely slang, musical and pop culture references all while teaching you strong leadership and relationship lessons along the way.

[PURCHASE BOOK]   [KINDLE VERSION]

SUCCESS IS IN YOUR HAND
19 Keys To Unlocking The Successful Person You Were Designed To Be

In Book One of Ryan C. Greene's "Purpose, Power, Passion Series", Success Is In Your Hand is your handbook for reaching your full potential, fulfilling your purpose and developing yourself into the successful person God designed you to be. This book is full of 19 easy to learn concepts that can quickly be applied to help you excel in your personal and business life. The book also includes a 21-Day Workbook Companion which takes you through each key to unlocking your success.

[PURCHASE BOOK]   [KINDLE VERSION]

Are you ready to make a living doing what you love by becoming a Passionpreneur? If so, enroll in the Passionpreneur Starter Lab at **www.PassionpreneurAcademy.com**

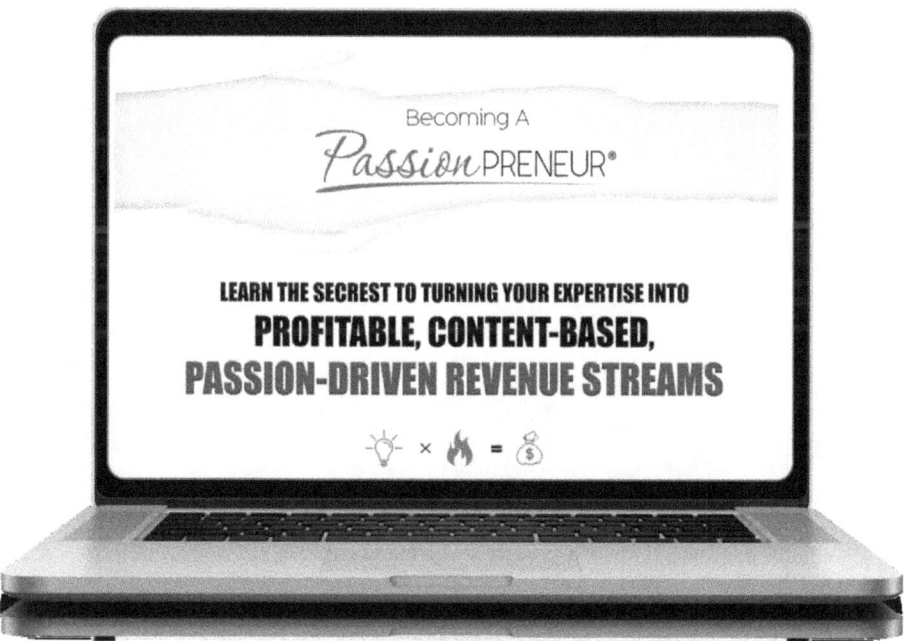

www.ingramcontent.com/pod-product-compliance
Lightning Source LLC
Chambersburg PA
CBHW021848090426
42811CB00033B/2181/J